D1087842

MASTERING PIANO TECHNIQUE
A Guide for Students, Teachers, and Performers

MASTERING PIANO TECHNIQUE
A Guide for Students, Teachers, and Performers

Seymour Fink

With illustrations by Donald G. Bell

AMADEUS PRESS
Reinhard G. Pauly, General Editor
Portland, Oregon

Corrected reprint 1993

ISBN 0-931340-46-2
Printed in Singapore.

AMADEUS PRESS
9999 S. W. Wilshire, Suite 124
Portland, Oregon 97225

Library of Congress Cataloging-in-Publication Data

Fink, Seymour.
   Mastering piano technique : a guide for students, teachers, and
performers / Seymour Fink ; with illustrations by Donald G. Bell.
     p.   cm.
   Includes bibliographical references and index.
   ISBN 0-931340-46-2
   1. Piano-Instruction and study.   I. Title.
MT220.F44 1992
786.2'193-dc20   •91-48342
                                                       CIP
                                                        MN

To Carole Fink

Contents

Preface 9

Introduction 11

Overview 13

Definitions 16

Part One **Fundamental Movements** 21

Section 1 **Introduction** 22

Section 2 **Posture and Primary Arm Movements** 24
PM 1 Postural Alignment 24
PM 2 Arm Extension With Pronation 24
PM 3 Shoulder-Girdle Movement and Pendulum Swing 27
PM 4 Rotation of Arm and Shoulder Girdle 29
PM 5 Forearm Push Stroke 31
PM 6 Lateral Motion 33

Section 3 **Primary Hand and Finger Movements** 36
PM 7 Hand Positions and Finger Strokes 39
PM 8 Hand Scoop 40
PM 9 Pulling Fingers 42
PM 10 Unfolding Fingers 44

Section 4 **Integrative Movements** 46
IM 1 Adapting Shoulder and Arm Movements to the Keyboard 46
IM 2 Adapting Hand and Finger Movements to the Keyboard 48
IM 3 Adapting Playing Mechanism to the Keyboard—Arm Cycling 50

Section 5 **Movements Shaped by the Piano** 53
5 A Posture at the Keyboard 53
5 B The Shape of and Relations Within the Keyboard 57
5 C The Pedals 66

Section 6 **Summary** 71

Part Two **Applied Movements** 73

Section 7 **Introduction** 74

Section 8 **Upper Arms and Shoulder Girdle** 76
8 A Pulling Arm Legato—Pronating and Supinating Circles 78
8 B Pushing Arm Strokes—Short and Long Sounds 83
8 C Upper-Arm Gravity Drops 87
8 D Multi-Note Arm Patterns—Finger Stretching 90

Contents

Section 9 **Forearms** 96

    9 A Forearm Bounce on Palm Finger—Correspondence 96

    9 B Lateral Forearm Skip 101

    9 C Forward Gravity Drops—Rebounds 102

Section 10 **Hands** 106

    10 A Hand Bounce 106

    10 B Scoop Chords 110

Section 11 **Thumbs** 112

    11 A Thumb Movement—Adduction and Flexion 112

    11 B Collapsing Midjoint—Lateral Thumb Movement 114

    11 C Flexibility and Correspondence 116

Section 12 **Fingers 2 Through 5** 118

    12 A Pulling Finger Strokes 118

    12 B Collapsing Fifth Fingers—Lateral Strength 123

    12 C Overlapping Legato 126

    12 D Unfolding Finger 129

    12 E Sidesaddle Walking—Substitution Practice 132

Section 13 **Summary** 136

Part Three **Synthesized Movement** 139

Section 14 **Introduction** 140

Section 15 **Legato Movements** 142

    15 A Joggle Movement—Chordal Repetition 142

    15 B Forearm-Finger Grouping 148

    15 C Upper-Arm Gesturing—Cycles 152

    15 D Finger Length Adaptations 158

Section 16 **Lateral Movements** 160

    16 A Lateral Extension—Preparation Shifts 160

    16 B Walking Rebounds—Parallel Motion—Octaves 163

    16 C Fake Legato 168

Section 17 **Release Movements** 171

    17 A Hand Releases 171

    17 B Hand-Finger Staccato 171

    17 C Finger Releases 173

Section 18 **Summary** 176

Conclusion 177

Glossary 178

Suggestions for Further Reading 183

Index 185

Preface

I first thought about writing a book on piano technique many years ago when, as a young professor at the Yale School of Music, I had difficulty finding books on technique that could give practical, long-term guidance to those in need of it. Such a book, dealing developmentally with the physical side of playing, would spur musical growth and free lesson time for a deeper study of literature and interpretation. I have discovered two things in the intervening thirty years: such a book is not written quickly; and no one has yet done it in just the way I had hoped.

And so you are now holding the book I would have assigned to my students years ago, and all along. I have written it also to give teachers the comprehensive perspective and certainty of approach they need to successfully guide their students' technical growth and improve their own playing as well. Intended as a practical book for extended study (self or assigned), it identifies and develops the movements which pianists must make to satisfy and enlarge their musical imaginations. It is not a book about music literature or interpretation per se, but it is thoroughly committed to the beauty and power of music in performance.

My conclusions on the what, when, and how of piano technique have evolved slowly through my long and rich experience as a pianist, and more important, as a pedagogue. I cannot pinpoint where particular ideas have come from, though I have learned much from others: from my teachers, my students, and in animated conversations with friends and colleagues. In extensive reading on the subject, I have found three seminal books to which I am particularly indebted: Ortmann, *The Physiological Mechanics of Piano Technique;* Schultz, *The Riddle of the Pianist's Finger;* and Pichier and Krause, *The Pianist's Touch.* I have experimented in my own playing and teaching, especially to discover valuable pedagogic insights and avenues. But mostly I have learned from the sheer observation of piano playing (great and not so great) over many years— by listening and looking, analyzing and remembering.

Much less vague in my mind are the contributions of the many wonderful and patient people who have helped me with this project. To these friends and colleagues who have read the book at various stages, I wish to express my sincere gratitude for their uniquely helpful reactions: Roger Peltzman, Stephen Zank, George Manos of the National Gallery of Art, John Pidgeon, Professor N. Jane Tan of Towson State University, Professor Ray Hanson of The Hartt School of Music, Professor Ann Koscielny of the University of Maryland, and Professor Mark Wait of the University of Colorado.

At an early and critical stage, Professor George Kiorpes of the University of North Carolina at Greensboro read the manuscript and encouraged me to persevere. My long-term colleague at the State University of New York (SUNY) at Binghamton, Professor Walter Ponce, has stimulated and enriched my perceptions through twenty years of continuing conversation about music, piano teaching, and piano playing, and (more than he knows) through my close observation of his prodigious physical and artistic gifts. The existence of this book in its final form owes much to the dedicated mentorship of another colleague at SUNY, Professor Edith Borroff who, taking me under her wing, shared freely of her splendid expertise about writing and form, and lent immeasurable time, energy, and wisdom in guiding me through the brambles of realizing my vision.

The musical examples have been deftly realized through the computer talents of David Agard of Binghamton, New York. I also want to express my deep appreciation to Professor Donald Bell of the SUNY Binghamton Art Department, who created the many fine illustrations that make this book so much more clear and attractive. I have found my association with the Amadeus Press all that I might have hoped for, and wish to thank particularly Robert Conklin, publisher; Richard Abel, editor-in-chief; Elizabeth Franken and Linda Willms, my editors; their care and tactful expertise have greatly improved the work. And finally, I want to thank my wife Carole Fink, to whom this book is dedicated, for her loving concern, her perceptive help and encouragement, and for the ongoing and boundless inspiration she has provided me during the thirty-year gestation of the book.

Seymour Fink
State University of New York
Binghamton, New York 13902

Introduction

Piano technique is more than the physical ability to render the printed page of music accurately; it is the vehicle for interpretation, the key to musical expression. Movement and meaning are so closely related to each other that the specific character of the gesture is itself part of the message conveyed. For example, musical continuity demands physical continuity, it being virtually impossible to express a quiet, flowing line with either constricted or overly energetic movement. Likewise, rhythmic vitality can be articulated only through vigorous action. Technical decisions are thus never made in an artistic vacuum. But having said this, I must also add that there is no single correct way to play. Good technical training encourages exploration of a variety of approaches for, by encouraging flexibility, efficiency, and surety—whatever the artistic purpose, performers become freer to follow their imaginations. In short, when pianists are confident in their ability to create something extraordinarily beautiful at the keyboard, they dare to try. And only by trying can they succeed.

Technique is like grammar; once it is a part of you, you speak without conscious attention to it. In the same way, technical matters function below the conscious level in mature pianists. Experimenting first one way then another, pianists mine their deepest, most intuitive feelings about the music, seeking out a particular mood, tone color, or expressive nuance. Ultimately their inner musical thinking triggers the requisite movement so they experience no separation between muscular exertions and musical goals.

The circumstances of the novice differ radically from those of the seasoned player; consistent technical training must be made an integral part of the learning experience. When first coming to grips with the relatively awkward conditions surrounding purposeful movement at the keyboard, students should be instructed in a healthy and efficient use of their bodies. Poor technical training slows their rate of progress and inevitably limits pianistic growth. Clearly, pianists and piano teachers can profit from a graphic, practical, and comprehensive treatment of the biomechanics and pedagogy of piano technique, its means and ends, presented in a cogent, organized manner.

What can piano teachers impart to their students in the period of early study about the physical side of playing? They can first make students aware of their movement patterns, both the helpful and harmful. Second, instructors can advise students about posture, efficiency of movement, habit formation (the systematic progression from consciously to subconsciously informed movement), learning strategies, various kinds of simple and combined coordinations, keyboard shape and tactics, and instrumental mechanics. Furthermore, teachers can demonstrate how these relate to serious music making. Students at all levels are capable of increasing their awareness and objectifying their knowledge of their own movements, learning new coordinations, improving their analytic and problem-solving skills, and increasingly

Introduction

forging those indispensable links between technique and musical conception—all the while cultivating efficacious practice habits.

These are in essence the reasons for which I first devised and subsequently tested and modified the exercises, both mental and physical, contained in this book. The book presents the basic biomechanics of playing, those uses of the body that are as fundamental to the beginner as to the professional. In addition, this book lays out an orderly program for acquiring these tangible skills. In the absence of reliable guidance, technical development is not only often haphazard, but bad habits can become so ingrained as to frustrate the music-making objectives of which a student is otherwise capable. Sadly, far too many promising pianists (including some accomplished artists) are thwarted by purely physical problems. Physicians and physical therapists who work with pianists suffering occupational injuries will find the book a useful resource about the kinds of movements pianists need to make, and how these movements might best be learned.

One of my objectives has been to provide a large number of advantageous coordinations, for the more varied the performer's technical palette, the more ways to efficiently and gracefully manage the keyboard, the greater the potential range of expression. We have all experienced the frustration of striving to achieve musical objectives which prove to be beyond our bodies' present abilities; I hope to reduce, if not eliminate, the palpable causes contributing to this limitation on expressivity. Above all, I wish to stress adaptability, for pianists are repeatedly challenged to adjust immediately to differing pianos, rooms, climates, moods, associated musicians or musical groups, as well as to their own spontaneous artistic inspiration. We are called upon instantly, often unconsciously, to produce those gestures that breathe life and meaning into our music making. In such circumstances the physical means must be so thoroughly grounded as to become one with the conceptual ends being served.

This book is aimed at both the conscientious teacher and the serious piano student; it not only explains what must be learned, but provides the means of doing so. Piano teachers, whether teaching privately or in an institutional setting, will find this practical, comprehensive treatment of piano technique valuable as a supplemental assignment within the normal private study curriculum. Students will have in a single volume the information and guidance necessary for long-term technical growth. Teachers or students can either work through the book systematically, or turn to particular sections in order to address specific problems. I have also tried to structure this book in a way to make it a useful textbook for piano pedagogy courses offered to students planning teaching careers. Finally, I hope it will function as a useful database of technical information and pedagogic insight, and thus serve as a guide to a variety of physical approaches to the instrument.

Overview

As the reader embarks upon this technical journey, I wish to share some thoughts about its goals and processes. In performance our minds project a musical conception, while our bodies produce the purposeful movement that brings it to life. This book is about the coherent development of this purposeful movement. Think of technique as more than pressing the right key at the right time; rather, conceive of it as a dancer might, as the avenue to expressiveness and beauty. Grace, efficiency, power, coordination, flexibility, fluidity, and line— these are the qualities that bear upon technical growth and development.

I believe that the central focus of technical study is the movement mechanics of the player's body: the way it is positioned, the way it functions, the sensations it feels, and the movements it produces. The pianist practices to acquire the habits that will create the musical meanings he or she seeks. As in the case of a golf or tennis swing, pianistic movement can be analyzed and its elements separated, but the component motions, once separately mastered, must be reintegrated to produce a higher level of proficiency. The widely held notion that technique largely concerns the learning of recurring keyboard patterns such as scales and arpeggios is, I hold, far too narrow. This notion merely begs the question, for these keyboard patterns may be played with widely different technical approaches, each with its own usefulness.

The body must first be taught to establish and maintain excellent posture, creating the efficient skeletal alignment that promotes economical, balanced muscle use. It should also function in a healthy, centered balance, its two sides evenly developed. This view implies, at least in the beginning, bilateral, mirrored movements in contrary motion. The weakness on one side typically accompanying normal right- or left-handedness, persists indefinitely if the student does not consciously intervene. Uneven development is also fostered by the traditional literature, which typically asks more complicated things of the right hand than it does of the left. And last, the common practice of extensive parallel playing often exacerbates the problem.

The larger members and movements of the playing apparatus must first be identified and mastered, with smaller ones following progressively. I therefore move from general posture, to shoulder-girdle movement, to the arms, hands, and, finally, fingers. Concentrating primarily on finger movement at the beginning of any program of technical training leaves much to chance, for playing uses the whole mechanism in graceful, integrated movement; fingers, its smallest members, are essentially a part of the larger movement patterns.

I am convinced that the mind and body must be trained together. Students should develop a keen sense of physical self-awareness, one that can read and respond to inner kinesthetic signals. This can best be accomplished by learning to work calmly, with minimal tension, and by carefully analyzing, temporarily isolating, and systematically mastering the core movements of piano playing. Thus in Part One, I present what I call the ten Primary Movements of playing in a format that is intentionally unrelated to the normal position at the piano; I do so to encourage fresh thinking, to reduce the interference of old habits, and to focus complete attention on the essential movements themselves.

I believe that focusing on the body's movements with their inner kinesthetic sensations creates the condition of awareness, flexibility, and refinement that allows the performing pianist to physically mirror and reproduce the finely tuned nuances of musical thought. Technical development implies the ability to accomplish this with greater and greater subtlety and power. In effect, pianists are dancer-athletes of the keyboard: to perform is to move in ways that give birth to the products of musical imagination. The greater the command of physical techniques—the greater the number of ways available to move with grace, efficiency, elegance, power, subtlety, and control—the greater the meaning and emotion communicated to the listener. Such is the nature of creativity in performance.

I offer a word—a word of both caution and hope: this is not a book to be read casually, in one or even several sittings; it must be read slowly and worked with carefully, a little at a time. From the printed word and static illustrations the reader must conceptualize the intended elements, positions, and movements. Descriptions are in many cases complex and directions hard to follow. Reading, even with complete intellectual understanding, is insufficient; only turning the ideas into action will complete the study of the book.

Genuine kinesthetic learning, which is essentially the development of new habits, takes place only through repeated experience: mind and body work and progress together. Each reader, with growing experience, gains a sense of what personally works best. Each student will learn the most effective way to promote the process of conscious habit formation, how large to start a gesture, the number of repetitions, when to decrease movement size or increase tempo, and in general, how far a specific coordination can be improved in any one work session. Work sessions should be kept short, though several in one day are certainly possible, even desirable. Two fifteen-minute sessions are better than a single half-hour session. Some coordinations grow on one only slowly, requiring several days, or even weeks of gentle, intermittent application. Many sessions should be devoted solely to improving older coordinations at various stages of development.

New exercises should be tackled when one feels "ready," but I advise not trying to learn more than one new coordination at a time. Do not race through the exercises, rather savor them; a great deal of benefit is gained from proceeding slowly. Try each new position, movement, and direction immediately upon mention and then carefully monitor the outcome. Beginners are more likely to use the book under the guidance of a teacher. Advanced students may use the book working on their own, as well as with a teacher. Old responses must sometimes be consciously inhibited, to prepare the mind and body for new and initially strange-feeling movement patterns. Proceed slowly, calmly, and thoughtfully, and in the prescribed order. Thorough knowledge can come only out of concentrated, if quasi-dissociated, mental effort, physical experience, thoughtful repetition, and perseverance.

Of course students will come to this study at different stages of their development and with a wide variety of backgrounds and length of experience. It is impossible to make a statement about the length of time students should be working with the book. But certainly the exercises are conceived in a long arc of progress, and I can well imagine the work of absorbing the various movements covered in the book to the point of their continued healthy and natural development taking a period of several years.

Artistry at the piano can never equal a sum of specifically learned technical skills. Rather, like dancers who continually work at the barre throughout their professional careers, pianists will work with the movements presented in the book until the patterns become a natural part of themselves; until they become part of their permanent warming-up and conditioning routines; and until they become an integral part of their musical conceptualization processes. Because the exercises stress variety and spontaneity, they will encourage the performer in the quest for a deeper understanding of the musical art.

Definitions

I have established a precise vocabulary for writing this book that accurately describes the various elements, positions, movements, and inner sensations involved in the act of playing. When common expressions are inexact or unavailable, I resort to technical terms to reduce ambiguity. Here are some examples:

1. The five fingers are numbered in the traditional way: thumbs are designated 1, index fingers are 2, middle fingers 3, ring fingers 4, and little fingers 5.

   The three *joints* and *bones of the fingers* are not differentiated in most books dealing with technique, but in this book they are considered separately **(Fig. 1-1)**. So starting with their connection to the hands, label the joints of fingers 2 through 5, knuckle joint (or just knuckle), midjoint, and nail joint. Again starting with their connection to the hands, label the bones, first, second, and third phalanx, or knuckle phalanx, midphalanx, and nail phalanx.

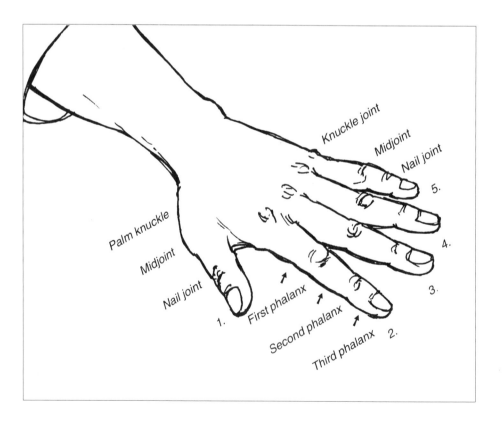

Figure 1-1. The hand, showing the three joints and three phalanxes of the fingers.

Designate the primary attachment of the thumbs to the hands near the undersides of the wrists the palm knuckle (carpo-metacarpal), followed by the midjoint, and lastly the nail joint. The three thumb phalanxes (bones) are called first, second, and third phalanx, or palm phalanx, midphalanx, and nail phalanx.

2. The *shoulder girdle,* a flexible, yokelike structure, is made up of collarbones and shoulder blades. Connected to the breast bone in front, and designed to float freely over the rib cage in a sea of muscle, its mobility promotes the wonderful freedom and range of movement of the upper arms **(Fig. 1-2).** The shoulder girdle is the first link in the piano-playing chain; it initiates, supports, and controls most of the length-adjusting and playing gestures of the arms.

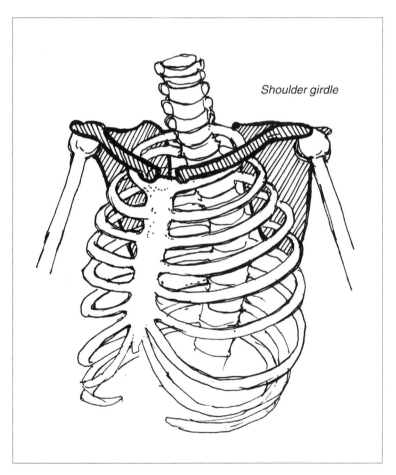

Shoulder girdle

Figure 1-2. The shoulder girdle—the first link in the chain of the piano-playing apparatus.

3. Two pairs of convenient terms describe the movement of the arms and hands. The first set, *pronation* and *supination,* refers to the direction of arm twisting **(Fig. 1-3)**: to pronate is to turn the arms inward towards the thumbs; to supinate is to twist in the opposite direction, as in turning the palms forward or upward.

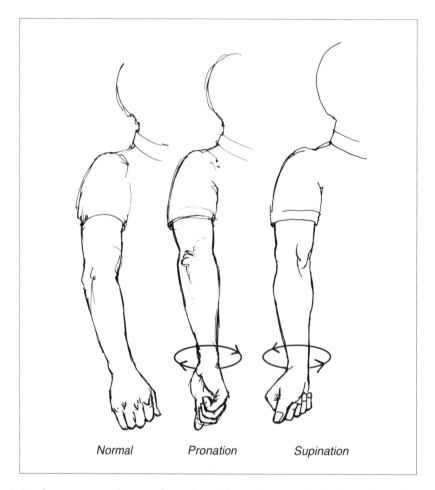

Figure 1-3. Arm pronation and supination—the two twisting directions.

The second pair of terms, *abduction* and *adduction,* refers to any lateral movement with reference to an imaginary vertical central line **(Fig. 1-4)**. To abduct upper arms is to hinge them outward at the shoulders away from the body's center; to adduct them is to return. To abduct hands, while in the normal playing position, is to shift them to the outside with thumbs pushing forward; to adduct them is to project fifth fingers forward, causing the wrists to bend outward.

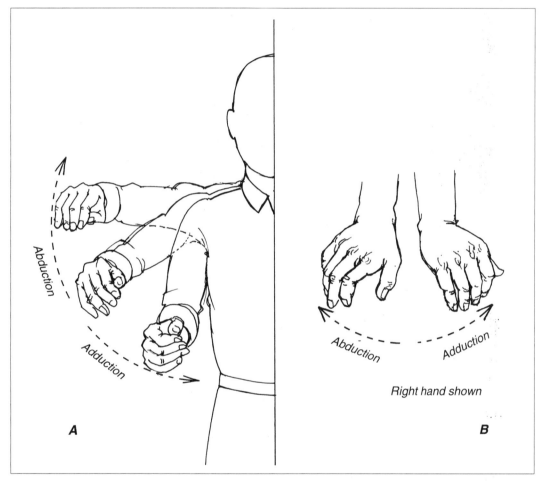

Figure 1-4. Abduction and adduction—moving away from and returning to the relevant medium plane: (A) the arm; (B) the hand.

4. Think of the *keyboard* as having three depth zones (**Fig. 1-5**): the *white* area is its near third up to the edge of the black keys. The *black* area refers to the back two-thirds adjacent to the fallboard, and includes the narrow part of the white keys. I use the term *gray* area to indicate an imaginary lateral band approximately one-inch wide that evenly overlaps their common border. Play in the gray area to minimize the in/out adjustments of the upper arms when moving single fingers laterally on note patterns involving both black and white keys. For example, one would try to touch both fingers in the gray area when playing quick chromatic octaves with 1 and 5.

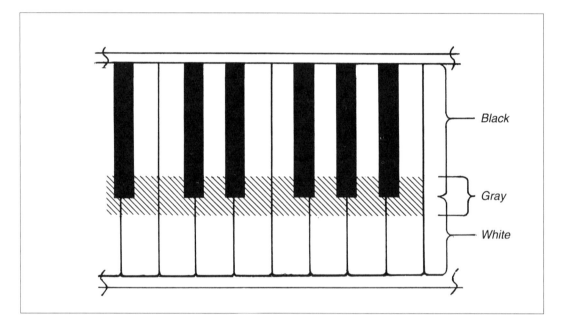

Figure 1-5. The three depth-zone areas of the keyboard—black, white, and gray. The gray zone overlaps the common border of the other two zones.

I refer to the physical and psychological center of the keyboard as middle D. A two-sided mirror placed lengthwise along D in the center of the piano reflects identical key patterns on both its sides. Performing contrary motion patterns centered on middle D allows our bodies to operate in a comfortably centered, bilaterally symmetrical mode, as well as to develop equal abilities on both its sides.

Part One **Fundamental Movements**

Section 1 **Introduction**

Part One of the book, Fundamental Movements, is devoted largely to those movements and concepts that I feel can best be taught away from the instrument. They include the following:

1. The ten primary movements that represent the core of essential piano-playing movement broken up into its component parts.
2. The three integrative movement patterns—learned away from the piano—to help you adapt these new movement habits to the normal position at the piano.
3. Sections on posture, keyboard shape, and pedals that lead you to acquire a healthful, intelligent approach to the instrument.

The ten primary movement exercises, which are presented first, are aimed at perfecting the basic movements required for piano playing. Beginning with posture and the larger units and movements of the shoulder girdle and arms, they progress to the smaller, more refined motions of the hands and fingers. The exercises are to be practiced away from the instrument in an expansive, relaxed state, and in a manner that encourages you to fully enjoy your temporary freedom from matters relating to keyboard shape, sound production, and musical meaning. Many readers will find this novel approach a boon to their understanding and development.

Some readers, however, many of them fine pianists who have worked intensively on technique at the instrument, may find it difficult to disassociate technique from the feel of a real keyboard and from the experience of live sound. I would encourage these readers to try extra hard, because for them the gains in objectivity and personal insight can be exceptionally rewarding. Nevertheless, for those persistently troubled by the lack of a piano, peeking ahead to relevant sections of Part Two before returning to pick up the thread might give a certain relief.

All readers with an urge to vary the diet slightly might work in Section 5 while working their way through Sections 2, 3, and 4. But, in general, I advise applying a calm, systematic approach, which is itself part of what must be learned for healthy technical development. Working thoughtfully away from the piano focuses your attention on your own body and temporarily away from musical and typographical concerns; this greatly increases your self-awareness, objectivity, and receptivity to new ideas. It also simplifies the goal of isolating and learning the anatomical parts of the playing mechanism with their various movements and interactions.

Stand before a mirror, if possible, in good postural alignment, with feet comfortably apart, and with sufficient surrounding space to swing your arms freely. Perform the exercises working both arms together in contrary motion, as this centers the body, promotes equal development of both its sides, and provides a basis for intelligent comparison. One hand or arm often masters a movement before the other, and so can serve as a model for its slower mate. Upon discovering an imbalance, as often happens, expend extra effort on the weaker side immediately to restore parity and balance between the two halves of the body.

Practice in short, 10–15 minute intervals several times a day, progressing through the exercises in order, as several short sessions of the same cumulative length are more valuable than one long session. Balance your attention between improving old movements and acquiring new ones. Begin an untried exercise deliberately with enlarged movements, using visual and kines-thetic feedback to monitor your actions. Notice how the mind and body interact. For instance, often the harder you try to concentrate on the task at hand, the greater the build-up of mental and physical tension—then the greater the interference to coordinated movement. To counter this, imagine yourself as a detached observer, merely noticing your repeated movements in an objective, unemotional, quasi-dissociated manner. Working in this way decreases inner tension and mental interference, and increases your capacity for control, coordinated movement, and habit formation. In short, learning is faster. With experience you will find an optimal balance between intensity of thought and casualness.

Repeat the new exercise until it begins to feel like an instinctively ingrained habit, when you can effect the correct movement without giving it the conscious scrutiny it demanded at first. The trajectory and speed of the movement now seem to proceed in a preprogrammed way, independent of conscious follow-up, freeing the mind to address a subsequent movement well before the completion of the present one. Increase the speed of the movement gradually, reducing its size, and eliminating extraneous muscular activity. Use a metronome to pace and record your progress. Take a leisurely period— perhaps four to six weeks—to learn and master the primary and integrative movements in Part One. Take additional time to complete the instrumental orientation work in Section 5.

Focus on the movements themselves, the way they look and feel, much as a dancer works. Delight in your freedom from other responsibilities. Counter any urge to try these movements at the piano; the new setting will help you give up old, less efficient habits that can be triggered by your normal position at the instrument. Progress (new habits) comes naturally, the result of calm, reflective repetition. Experience joy in motion for its own sake—its beauty, its grace, its increasing efficiency and apparent effortlessness—and especially in its potential for expression. You will be laying the groundwork for a first-rate piano technique.

Learning new behavior patterns involves deliberately making the conscious unconscious and discarding the unnecessary.

Section 2 **Posture and Primary Arm Movements**

Section 2, a unit devoted to posture and to the arms, includes the first six primary movements. These exercises focus on the overall position of the body and on the basic building blocks of arm movement in a proficient piano technique.

Primary Movement 1 **Postural Alignment**

Begin all exercises in this book with good postural alignment, this being the first habit to ingrain. To do so

1. Release (relax) the muscles of the back of your neck to allow your head to move and balance forward and upward, creating a sense of space between it and your body.
2. Feel your torso lengthen following your head upwards as the curves of the spine elongate. While moving upward, avoid augmenting natural lower back sway by releasing (widening) the lower back muscles and gently contracting the lower abdominal muscles.
3. Release your shoulders to fall downward and outward to the sides. Your shoulders will find their correct position automatically once the torso-neck-head alignment is established and balanced. The ideal shoulder notch is slightly forward of the sides, with the shoulder blades comfortably spread. Your spine will feel as though it is stretching upward through your shoulder girdle which has been released (widened outward) in response to the force of gravity.

This position eliminates unnecessary tension and encourages an easy, efficient use of the body. Learn it well and assume it automatically before doing any of the other exercises in the book.

Primary Movement 2 **Arm Extension With Pronation**

Now, standing with the postural alignment described in PM 1, allow the arms to hang freely, elbows slightly bent and hands forming loose fists. Perform the following two movements simultaneously:

1. Extend your arms downward, the thumbs pointing and pushing toward the floor; and
2. Twist the arms inward (while extending) until your elbows lock at the completion of the extension, at which point the shoulders begin curling inward and the palms face first backward, then outward. This turning toward the thumb is called *pronation* **(Fig. 1-6)**.

3. Relax and untwist the arms which unlocks the elbows and returns you to your original position. This movement is called *supination*.

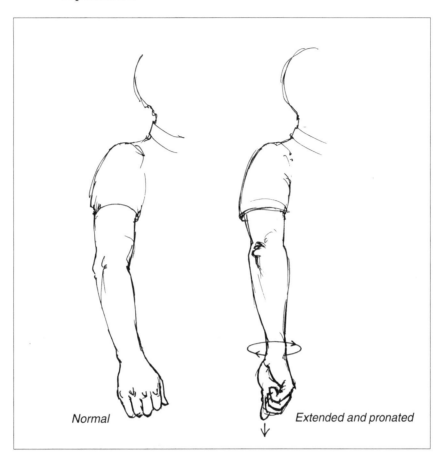

Normal | Extended and pronated

Figure 1-6. Arm extension with pronation (PM 2). Upper arms move slightly forward.

Throughout the exercise, the shoulder girdle, released and widened to the outside, serves to stabilize the lengthened spine and to free movement in the shoulders.

Pronation and arm extension have a natural affinity, even though it is possible to do one without the other. Executed together, which in this exercise here feels like pressing and turning imaginary thumbtacks, clockwise with your left thumb, counterclockwise with your right, they produce an assertive, thrusting gesture. When boxers punch, their arms pronate as they extend, the pronation increasing the impact. Pronation increases the impact for pianists too. Conversely, supination typically accompanies release, retraction, and transition.

Practice single arm extensions using the rhythmic patterns outlined in **Figure 1-7**. Stand with good postural alignment; extend and pronate your arms with thumbs pointing toward the floor, stopping the pronation when your arms become straight. Hold for two counts at MM 88, then release for two counts. Repeat a half dozen times, observing the simultaneous extending and twisting, and its release **(Fig. 1-7A)**. Next, hold for one count and release for three counts **(Fig. 1-7B)**. Finally, while remaining in the basic tempo, extend for increasingly shorter periods and lengthen the release time between each **(Fig. 1-7C)**, producing slow, but sharply pointed staccato thrusts. The release (recoil) position automatically becomes the starting point for the next stroke; avoid any additional wind-up or preparatory moves. To make the shortest strokes sufficiently sharp, throw rather than press the arms, for without this ballistic impulse, well completed before the arms reach their greatest extension, releases are sluggish. The darting, almost disembodied movement is like a snake's tongue; the body remains centered, aligned, and quiet throughout. Do extra exercises with the weaker or slower arm until the arms feel equalized.

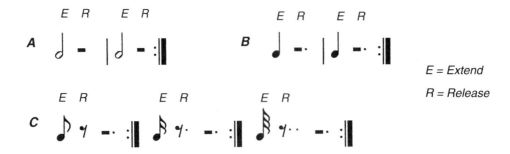

Figure 1-7. **Rhythmic exercise pattern for pronation extension.**

When these pronation-extensions feel reasonably automatic, perform them pointing forward at shoulder height without changing your original postural alignment—shoulders down and released to the outside. The psychological trick of thinking your thrown hands are leading the arm motion helps to prevent tensing or raising the shoulders any more than necessary. Notice how your shoulder blades separate and return to support each thrust; imagine twisting thumbtacks into a wall, then hitting a punching bag. Perform extensions at various angles between the vertical and the horizontal planes with your thumbs pointing the direction. Remember that normal playing takes place at about a 35° angle.

This group of exercises demonstrates the inherent advantages in speed and power realized by merging the separate elements of extension and pronation. While strengthening your upper arm, chest, and back muscles, they also serve to equalize and vastly increase the speed and dexterity of movement in your shoulder girdle, shoulders, and upper arms. The ability to move your arms with speed and accuracy is the linchpin of a good piano technique.

Primary Movement 3 **Shoulder-Girdle Movement and Pendulum Swing**

Stand again in good postural alignment—with your torso, neck, and head floating upwards, your shoulders released to the outside and falling slightly forward, and your arms hanging freely—with the palms of your hands brushing near the outsides of your legs. Lift (shrug) your shoulders as high as possible, hold them in that position for a moment, then let them fall. Repeat this vertical movement, accomplished by muscles in your neck and upper back, several times only to consciously learn to avoid it while exercising hereafter; there is no physical or expressive need to lift the shoulders while playing the piano.

Next, round your shoulders forward carrying your palms towards the front of your legs. Return beyond your original position to proceed in the reverse direction, forcing the tips of your shoulder blades towards one another with palms now touching the back of your legs. Repeat this back-and-forth cycle a dozen times keeping your shoulders down and noticing when they pass their normal released-to-the-outside notch. Work to increase the range, speed, and control of the movement, developing the muscles of the trunk and shoulders that make this action possible.

Small movements of the shoulder girdle are magnified in playing by the length of the arms as the shoulder girdle initiates and supports the arms' playing and reaching movements. This first major link in the playing mechanism needs serious attention both physically and kinesthetically. Accustom yourself to resuming the notched, slightly forward, released-to-the-sides neutral position of the shoulder girdle when returning from both the forward and reverse motions; this position stabilizes your lengthened spine and frees the upper arm movement associated with the shoulders.

Closely related to shoulder-girdle movement is the pendulum swing, an exercise in which the arms swing pendulumlike to create an extensive but passive movement in the shoulder girdle. To begin the exercise, stand with good postural alignment, arms hanging loosely by your sides, hands again forming loose fists. Firm (fix) your wrists and elbows just enough (no more) to keep your arms moving as a unit. Swing your arms backward, then forward in a loose pendulum motion, gradually increasing the range until the hands reach over your head in front (**Fig. 1-8**). Insure that your shoulders remain down and released to the outside through the length of the exercise. Make the downward pull of the cycle the primary action, and the upswing a follow-through. Swing through a dozen complete cycles concentrating on the extensive, relaxed movement of the shoulder girdle and shoulder joints.

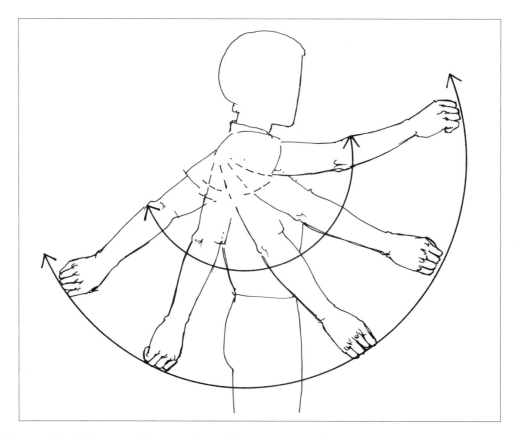

Figure 1-8. The pendulum swing (PM 3). Upper arms pull backward, then follow through forward.

Returning to a position of good postural alignment, pronate your arms slightly beyond the position in which knuckles face forward. Repeat the exercise a dozen cycles; your hands will tend to close in the forward movement and open on the backward movement as they seek an easier level of muscular tension. Occasionally stop to hold your arms horizontally, both in front and in back, for a count of 10. This strengthens upper arm and trunk muscles.

Finally, combine the pendulum swing with the rotation cycle, linking pronation to the downward pull and relative supination to the upward follow-through. The arms must swing and twist from the shoulder, in a strong and orderly, yet loose, fashion. Pendulum swings serve to increase the range and freedom of movement in the shoulder and shoulder girdle, elements essential for power, ease, sonority, and endurance. Pendulum swings may also be employed to stretch and relax the neck, back, chest, and shoulder muscles whenever concentrated practicing leads to a feeling of tension or tiredness.

Primary Movement 4 **Rotation of Arm and Shoulder Girdle**

The concern of this exercise is not with extension, but rather with an even, back-and-forth pronation-supination cycle. Position yourself in what you now know to be the standard preliminary position with head balanced forward and upward, spine lengthened, shoulders released to the outside, and arms hanging loosely. Center your arms on your straightened second and third fingers which are pressed lightly together and pointed towards the floor; extend the outside fingers away from this center (**Fig. 1-9**).

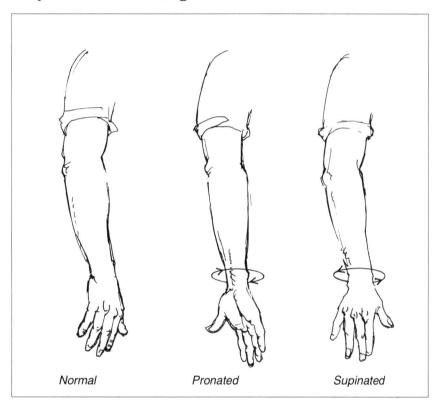

| Normal | Pronated | Supinated |

Figure 1-9. The rotation cycle (PM 4), consisting of a single pronating twist and a returning supinating twist.

Moving both arms at the same time, set up a loose, even rotation cycle starting at MM 88, fitting pronation to the beat. Increase speed gradually over several days to MM 160, working particularly on the less well-coordinated arm. Now reverse the movement, matching supination to the beat, a playing situation just as likely to occur as the first.

Next, perform two cycles to a single impulse, starting at MM 60, increasing your speed gradually to MM 100. Renew the impetus with tiny arm extension accents that propel the next pair of cycles forward. Adapt pronation to the beat, then supination, working always to equalize the actions and feelings between the arms.

Increasing the velocity of this and other movements is an important objective of most exercise programs. The following procedure **(Fig. 1-10)** which I call a *clustering routine* will help you gain mental and physical control of a quickened pace without forcing. A cluster is a combination of movements which are melded together by practice to the point that they can be psychologically treated as a single element.

Figure 1-10. Clustering practice routine for increasing velocity—a mental changing of gears.

1. Choose the number of movements in the cluster unit. For our purposes here I suggest two rotations, that is, two complete pronation-supination cycles **(Fig. 1-10A)**.
2. Accustom yourself to the sensation of grouping exactly two rotations to a single beat by alternating a beat consisting of two rotations with a beat of rest **(Fig. 1-10B)**.
3. Increase the speed of the cluster unit gradually.
4. After you have significantly increased your speed, work then to incrementally increase the number of cluster units performed in a row without the rest, from two to a much larger number **(Fig. 1-10C)**.

Balance the practice devoted to increasing speed within a single cluster with rotations aimed at simple, steady continuity. Reinforce the accents with tiny extension impulses, but never force the movements. From time to time reverse directions to become adept at matching pronation or supination to the beat. Make certain both arms act and feel alike.

Observe how your movements become finer, more limited in space, and seemingly looser as the speed increases. These results come from reducing the size of the movement and eliminating extraneous muscular activity. The single most important physical factor affecting increased velocity is that of diminishing the range of the movement. Also, the mere willing of double rather than single cycles spontaneously increases the potential for speed. Clustering thus acts as a kind of mental changing of gears. Gain experience with grouping three, then four rotations to a cluster unit, working to perfect fast, loose, controlled vibrations in both rotary directions. Mastery of these rotary movements allows you to support your fingers to great advantage in various tremolo and alternating patterns. Quickly applied single rotary action often backs individual tones in middle-speed melodic playing.

Primary Movement 5 **Forearm Push Stroke**

Stand in the usual position, arms hanging freely, hands in loose fists. Flex your forearms from the elbows as far as possible without moving your upper arms. Your hands should reach approximately shoulder height. Firm your wrists and fingers just enough to allow them to move as a unit with the forearms.

Next, slowly and completely unfold your arms as though you were working the slides of two imaginary trombones pointed horizontally forward **(Fig. 1-11)**. To achieve a straight-line motion you must push your upper arms forward, and consequently upward as well. Note the large shoulder-girdle involvement. When your arms are fully unfolded, return them along the same path to the original flexed position. Do a dozen complete cycles to kinesthetically ingrain the trombone-slide motion. As needed, give the weaker or less well-coordinated limb extra attention; eventually both arms should act and feel alike.

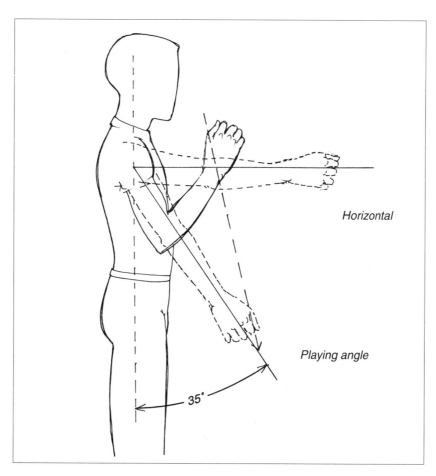

Horizontal

Playing angle

35°

Figure 1-11. The forearm push stroke—the trombone slide, straight-line diagonal approach to the keyboard (PM 5).

Now lower the imaginary trombones to fit the piano-playing angle of approximately 35°, an angle that can be readily observed in the forearm push stroke. With your arms together, do 20 large down/up forearm push strokes at MM 40. Do another 20, adding a rotary cycle that links pronation to the extension and supination to the return.

Maintain the pronated position to do shorter, faster strokes, using a *washboard motion* near the extended point of the arm's range (**Fig. 1-12**). Perform clusters of two strokes about three inches long to each beat at MM 72. Energize the beat to propel the next cluster forward by adding a further sharp but tiny pronation. Increase your speed gradually to MM 132 employing cluster practice principles. Then work with clusters of three and four strokes. The sustained pronated position tends to push the elbows outward, creating an extended, rounded shape to the arms that alters the angle of the forearm stroke. At a certain point this outward straying of the elbows must be compensated for at the piano by further pronation of the upper arms as you stroke in order to enter the key advantageously.

The forearm push stroke, a fundamental movement of playing, is both powerful and rapid since it uses the arm with no wrist movement and minimal elbow and shoulder action. It produces a forward friction on the surfaces of the key. This movement is most useful in playing both fast repeated notes and chords and in supporting ostinatolike finger patterns.

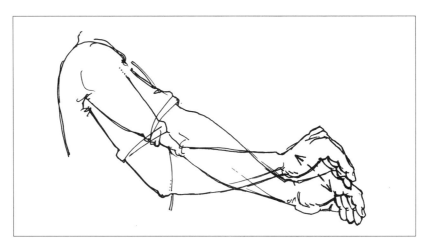

Figure 1-12. The forearm push stroke—washboard motion—the usable part of the trombone-slide diagonal with pronated arms.

Primary Movement 6 **Lateral Motion**

Stand in good postural alignment and flex your forearms upward until they are parallel with the floor. Hinging sideways, slowly raise your upper arms at the shoulders, keeping the elbow and wrist joints minimally fixed (**Fig. 1-13**). Allow only minimal shoulder-girdle support movement. At the top, the elbows are shoulder high and pointing to the sides with the palms facing the floor. Return your arms to their starting position, defining as wide an elbow arc as possible; repeat the motion several times, accustoming yourself to the lazy, flapping motion.

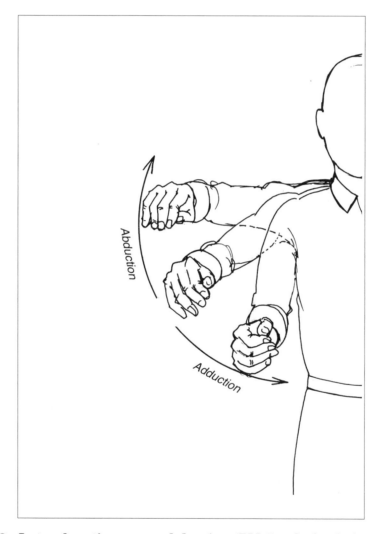

Figure 1-13. Lateral motion—arm abduction (PM 6)—the basis for moving sideways at the keyboard.

Next, in the raised elbow position, perform elbow circles generated by making small cycles with your shoulder girdle. Cycle 10 times in each direction, noticing the interaction between your upper arms and shoulder girdle. Next, circle 10 times in each direction while holding the arms completely straightened outward, fingers pointing to each side. These movements further strengthen the trunk and shoulder muscles. Work again for increased speed, range, and dexterity.

From the initial starting position of forearms parallel to the floor, flap the upper arms quickly outward; forearm pronation facilitates this. Pause at the top. Then snap your arms down; forearm supination helps here. Alternate these quick lateral movements, resting a few seconds between the change of direction. Sense the considerable mass moving with great rapidity in your shoulder and shoulder girdle, and become accustomed to the supportive rotary role of the forearms.

Finally, sit at a piano with the lid closed, and glide your hands in a pronated position from the center outward, returning along the same linear path; hook your thumbs over the edge of the lid to guide your arms in a straight-line motion. The upper arms and shoulder girdle lead and control the movement in both directions; forearms and hands follow. Insure that your arms look and feel alike as you execute this easily willed but complex adjustment in arm length, which is a recognizable and essential playing movement. Intersperse some arm flap exercises to underscore the importance of the upper-arm and shoulder-girdle movements involved.

As your hands glide back and forth over the closed piano lid, blend in the following additional movements:

1. Increase arm pronation as you move outward; increase supination on your return. This serves to keep knuckle lines level with the keyboard.
2. Moving sideways in the wrist, adjust your hand angles to keep the knuckle lines parallel with the fallboard: wrists move outward (hand adduction) as arms move to the outside; wrists move inward (hand abduction) as arms return to center.

These movements increase elasticity of the hand, keep the knuckle line parallel to the level keyboard, and maintain the hand facing straight-on so all its fingers can reach anywhere along the line. Players often forget that when the arms are spread apart it is the upper arms that initiate the change of direction to lead the movement back towards the center; forearms and hands follow this lead. Eventually these movements will become a graceful, curvilinear figure-eight which indeed resembles the movement of a dancer and is the basic model for lateral arm movement. After habituating yourself to the slower motion, try some very large, quick leaps along the keyboard lid, remembering to support this with appropriate forearm twisting. Pause between movements. Speed, accuracy, and shoulder relaxation are enhanced if you imagine that your thrown hands are pulling or leading your arms.

The upper arms, both supported by and hinged on the shoulder girdle, negotiate most lateral movements from single notes and the thirds and fourths of scale playing through the octave shifts of arpeggios to larger jumps. Acting as a crane, they position and support the hands and fingers. Many seeming finger or hand malfunctions are in reality difficulties best solved by freeing the shoulder-girdle and upper-arm movement from the shoulder.

Section 3 Primary Hand and Finger Movements

Section 3, a unit devoted to the hands and fingers, consists of the final four primary movements. These exercises focus on the basic positions and core movements of the hands and fingers as they relate to a proficient piano technique. I have made easier the learning of these positions and movements by presenting them, to the extent possible, with the arms held in a neutral and relaxed, nonpronated state.

Playing the piano requires an infinite variety of hand and finger formations, angles, and movements. All of them can be meaningfully organized through the use of a functional scheme (**Fig. 1-14**), which interrelates the three primary hand positions with the two basic finger movements.

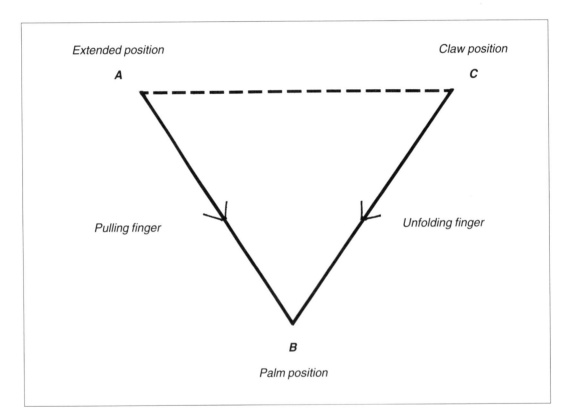

Figure 1-14. Diagram showing the theoretical relationship of the three primary hand positions to the two basic finger strokes (PM 7).

Hand position A. The extended position is, as the name implies, the aligning of all parts of the hand—fingers, thumbs, and palm in a flat plane—as, for example, when the hand is spread against a flat surface (**Fig. 1-15A**). The fingers are straightened and slightly spread, while the thumb is flattened back, separated from the rest of the fingers.

Hand position B. The palm position is derived from the extended position by bending (flexing) all the digits, including the thumbs, towards each other at the knuckles. Nail and midjoints flex minimally **(Fig. 1-15B)**. Lead with the shortest fingers—1, 2, and 5—fingers 4 and then 3 follow. The tips of the straightened fingers, now roughly perpendicular to the palms, form a rounded pattern: 1 touches 2 and 4 on their palm side, with 3 on top and 5 tucked under 4.

Note this position well, for it defines the hypothetical completion of virtually all finger strokes were they not cut short by the keyboard. That is to say, if the movements used to depress the keys are performed in the open air and extended to their logical conclusion, the hand would end in this position.

Hand position C. The claw position is derived from the extended position by flexing the nail and midjoints inward (under) while the knuckle joints remain still **(Fig. 1-15C)**. Be gentle, tightening your fingers no more than necessary to form the hands in this position. The long finger flexors, located under the forearms, control these actions by pulling through and tensing the wrists. Note that the thumbs also curve with their palm bones back, a position I call *claw thumbs*.

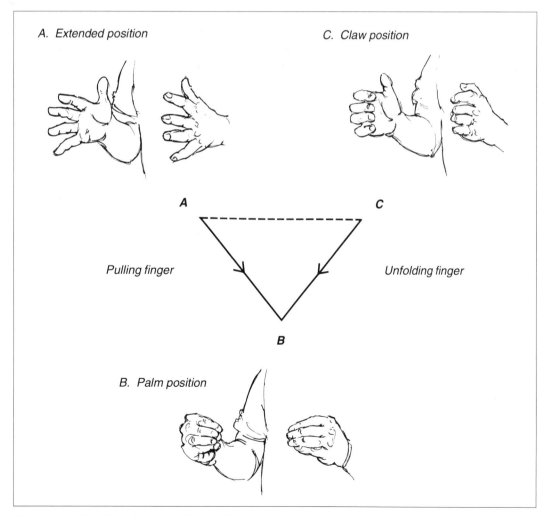

Figure 1-15. The three primary hand positions: (A) extended position; (B) palm position; and (C) claw position.

The two basic finger movements derive from opposing directional movements; the finger tips either pull under towards the palms, or they unfold away from the palms.

Finger stroke 1, the pulling finger. The fingers pull towards the palms as they move from the extended (A) to the palm position (B). Notice how the palm bones of the thumb, swinging from their palm knuckles under the wrists several inches behind the fingers, initiate their downward/inward swing.

Finger stroke 2, the unfolding finger. The fingers unfold as they move from the claw position (C) to the palm position (B); in unbending, their tips move perpendicularly away from the palms. The large knucklebone movement is generated by the small flexors located in the hand. The square look of many pianists' hands attests to the location of this specialized muscular development. Nail and midjoint movement tends to be reflexive, not the result of active extension.

Practice sufficiently to memorize the two basic finger strokes, doing each of them back and forth several dozen times. Note how each is formed in relation to the positions of the hand, their beginning and ending points: pulling fingers move from the extended position to the palm position, unfolding fingers move from the claw position to the palm position.

Primary Movement 7 **Hand Positions and Finger Strokes**

Practice the following exercises before a mirror with your hands in front of you. Starting from the usual standing position flex your nonpronated forearms at the elbows until your wrists are about chest level, where the hands and fingers, facing each other, can easily be seen and compared. The objectives here are to improve the directness and fluency of hand and finger movements and to bring the capabilities of the weaker hand up to those of the stronger hand.

PM 7.1 With hands in extended position (A), pull fingers to the palm position (B), retract them to the claw position (C), unfold fingers back out to the palm position (B), and then return to the original extended position (A). You have worked through the following hand-position pattern: A-B-C-B-A. Exaggerate the retraction of the thumbs in the claw and extended positions and the knucklebone flexion (straightening) of your fifth fingers in the palm position. Practice this setting-up exercise until it becomes second nature, working extra on the less well-coordinated hand. Then move on to the following exercises which require minimal finger independence.

PM 7.2 Starting in the claw position, hold your thumbs still while moving your other fingers through the patterns described in PM 7.1 above.

PM 7.3 Starting in the claw position, hold fingers 2, 3, 4, and 5 still while moving your thumbs through the patterns described in PM 7.1 above.

PM 7.4 Starting in the claw position, hold fingers 1 and 2 still while moving fingers 3, 4, and 5 through the patterns described in PM 7.1.

PM 7.5 Starting in the claw position, hold fingers 3, 4, and 5 still while moving fingers 1 and 2 through the patterns described in PM 7.1.

Work calmly and patiently, beginning slowly with as little tension as possible. Imagine yourself as a detached observer casually noting your finger movements. Be aware of what is happening, but avoid becoming too seriously involved—in learning movements like these, it often happens that the harder you try, the less control you have. Also, your fingers are probably not used to this extended range of movement. Use your better hand as a model for the less coordinated one, and stick with it until the original strangeness disappears, until the movements feel natural and you can quicken the pace, and until the two hands look and feel the same.

These few basic positions and movements are in fact the only ones involved in performing the exceedingly varied and complex hand and finger movements required in playing the piano. The exercises are designed to establish mental and physical control of these positions and movements, and to develop nimbleness, suppleness, equality between hands, some finger independence, and in general, substantial skill and dexterity in your finger movements.

Primary Movement 8 **Hand Scoop**

Stand in good postural alignment, your arms hanging freely. Draw your curved finger tips together, as though touching a flat surface, with thumbs pressing from the side; touch finger tips to the sides of your legs (**Fig. 1-16A**). Holding the elbows still, move (abduct) the upper arms outward several inches from the body, keeping the fingertips in contact with the leg by scooping your hands under at the wrists. The fingers remain fixed in relation to the hands as the hands slide under. Now return to the original position and slowly repeat this scooping motion a dozen times. Note the connection between the wrist and shoulder movements, between scooping hands and drifting arms. Memorize the sensations experienced from this movement in the shoulder girdle, arms, and wrists. I call this motion a *hand scoop* (**Fig. 1-16B**).

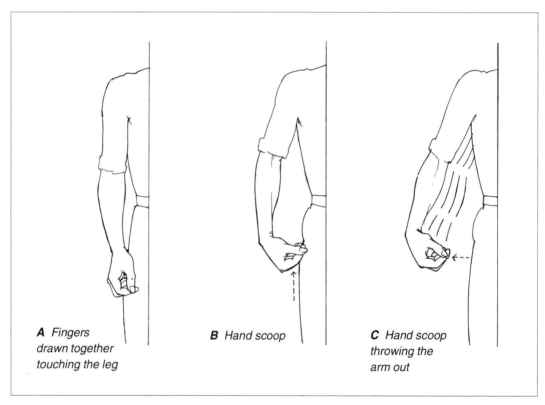

A Fingers drawn together touching the leg

B Hand scoop

C Hand scoop throwing the arm out

Figure 1-16. Hand scoop (PM 8)—the sophisticated mechanism for applying pulling-arm support to the fingers.

Once these motions feel reasonably ingrained, scoop more assertively until you feel it is your hand flexors on the undersides of your forearms that lead the movement pushing your arms outward. Note the pulling friction, relax, and return.

Augment the training value of this exercise by asking your hands to scoop against an increasingly reluctant arm. The use of this kind of counterpressure is called isometrics. Isometric training involves the conscious use of one muscle group against another with minimal movement for the purpose of increasing the workload of both muscle groups. Retain conscious control of the process, increasing the load only gradually and then only to a reasonable degree. Learn the value of optimal pacing with regard to the number of repetitions, their timing, and the assigned load. Become kinesthetically sensitive to the appearance of any tension or fatigue. Overstraining can slow progress and perhaps cause harm, something to watch especially when the muscle groups vary significantly in strength. Pace your effort so as to relax completely between each in/out movement to minimize tension and delay fatigue.

Finally, from the same starting position, scoop your hands under so abruptly that your arms, after a sharp countering press of their own, are kicked outward about five inches; relax and return **(Fig 1-16C)**. Repeat these punctuated, energetic scoops until you feel slight fatigue under your forearms.

Next, practice hand scoops using single finger pairs or various combinations of two, three, and four simultaneous fingers. Before scooping, loosely position unused fingers just off the leg in their most comfortable position, either raised minimally in front of the touching fingers, curved behind them, or a combination of the two. Choose from the following possibilities:

Any single finger pair.

Two-finger combinations:
1-2, 1-3, 1-4, 1-5, 2-3, 2-4, 2-5, 3-4, 3-5, 4-5.

Three-finger combinations:
1-2-3, 1-2-4, 1-2-5, 1-3-4,1-3-5, 1-4-5, 2-3-4, 2-3-5, 2-4-5, 3-4-5.

Four-finger combinations:
1-2-3-4, 1-2-3-5, 1-2-4-5, 1-3-4-5, 2-3-4-5.

The routine presents useful practice in forming the hand to various finger shapes. Note that all fingers, once the shape of the hand is set, move as "part of" the hand. The stroke is generated completely by hand flexion at the wrist, there being no independent finger movement in the knuckles. Hand and set fingers move as one unit.

This exercise integrates the scooping hand motion with necessary arm exertions. It also develops and highlights the role of hand flexion in piano technique, a role that is often overlooked even by mature pianists. The movement is used to play sharp, single notes and prepared chords and, as we shall see in Part Two, to create the light, flexible, and sustained arm-hand pressure needed to support a pulling-finger legato. Its role in the latter case can be spotted in the tendency of the wrists to rise when playing such passages.

Primary Movement 9 **Pulling Fingers**

Stand with good postural alignment, your arms hanging freely; press your palms lightly against your legs in the extended position **(Fig. 1-17A)**. Holding the wrists and elbows still, move (abduct) the arms outwards from your body several inches, maintaining leg contact with the fingertips by flexing fingers from their knuckles. At the end of the movement, the fingertips form the rounded palm position described in PM 7. Relax and return to the original position. Memorize this sliding motion, noting the change of the hands and fingers from a low to a high arch. Observe also the connection between knuckle and shoulder movements, between pulling fingers and drifting arms.

Now pull the fingers more assertively until you feel they lead the outward arm movement. I call this the *pulling finger* **(Fig. 1-17B)**. Note how the thumbs, moving from their palm knuckles under the wrists, pull across, not upward. The individual digits move almost as single units, which is the result of separate, graded pulls on each of their bones, not the result of stiffening. Knuckle flexion is the most pronounced, as the nail and midjoints flex minimally, just enough to maintain the basic original shape of the fingers.

Exercise the fingers isometrically by working them against a gently increasing arm pressure. Increase the isometric load gradually and to a lesser degree than that with hand scoops, as the pulling finger muscles are weaker than the scooping hand muscles. Pace your efforts so as to begin each pull from a completely relaxed extended position to minimize tension and fatigue.

Finally, pull the fingers under so suddenly that your arms, after a sharp countering press of their own, are kicked outwards about five inches **(Fig. 1-17C)**. I call this a *finger snap*. On the return, allow your hands to drift back to your legs in palm position before opening them to the original extended position. Repeat the action until it becomes habitual. Relax completely between efforts.

Next, do finger snaps with single pairs and then with various combinations of fingers as detailed in PM 8. Note that here, unlike hand scoops, the individual fingers actively and completely swing (flex) in their hand knuckles to create the movement. Make no attempt to achieve finger independence, but rather allow passive fingers, which have been placed loosely and minimally out of the way, to move freely with the active ones. Pace the repetitions to avoid or postpone any build-up of tension or fatigue.

Pulling fingers is one of the two basic finger coordinations used in piano playing. It is the movement of choice when called upon to produce moderate to fast, brilliant passage work. The fingers create backward friction with the keys as their tips move under towards the palms. They are supported by a sustained and flexible hand scoop pressure, which is itself backed by poised or pulling arms.

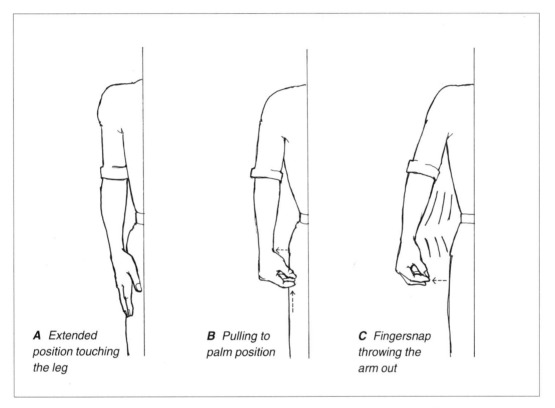

A *Extended position touching the leg*

B *Pulling to palm position*

C *Fingersnap throwing the arm out*

Figure 1-17. Pulling fingers (PM 9)—fingertips move towards the palm of the hands.

Primary Movement 10 **Unfolding Fingers**

Stand with good postural alignment, your arms hanging freely. Brush your legs with your hands in a loose (relaxed, not overly tense) claw position (**Fig. 1-18A**). Holding the wrists and elbows still, move (abduct) your arms outwards from your body, maintaining leg contact by unfolding fingers to palm position. Collapse your arches to return to claw position moving the entire arm as a single unit. Note the interplay between the highly active finger joints and the shoulders, between the unfolding/folding fingers and arms drifting out and in. Memorize these sensations from the shoulder girdle through the arms to the hands and fingers.

Gently and without strain unfold your fingers more assertively until you feel they lead the movement pushing your arms outward (**Fig. 1-18B**). I call this the *unfolding finger*. Note the pushing (forward) friction. Confine yourself to just a few gentle isometric exercises in this instance, as the relatively weak, small finger muscles located in the hand are a poor match for the large arm muscles. Start each new stroke from a relaxed claw position.

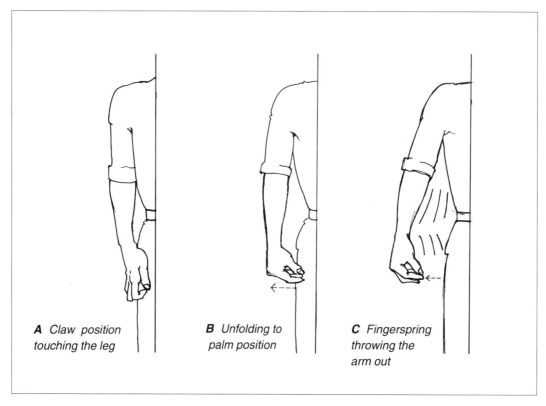

A Claw position touching the leg

B Unfolding to palm position

C Fingerspring throwing the arm out

Figure 1-18. Unfolding fingers (PM 10)—fingertips move away from the palm of the hands.

Finally, unfold your fingers so briskly that your arms, after a sharp, countering press of their own, are thrown outward; I call this the *finger spring* (**Fig. 1-18C**). Return your hands to your legs in palm position before collapsing to claw position. Concentrate on pushing off (springing) especially hard with fingers 1 and 5 and on relaxing several seconds between efforts.

Next, practice finger springs with single finger pairs and in combinations of two, three, and four fingers. Use the practice possibilities suggested in PM 8 for this purpose. Note the large movement in all three joints of the fingers, and the subtle and necessary integration with movements in the shoulder. Make no attempt at finger independence, allowing all passive fingers to move loosely with the active ones. Pace the repetitions to avoid or postpone any build-up of tension or fatigue.

Made exceedingly sensitive to key resistance by virtue of their proximity to the controlling small muscles in the hand, the unfolding fingers are especially valuable for executing fast, soft, and intricate legato patterns in distinction to those calling for brilliance, volume, or great spread. The forwardly poised arms with hanging hands (high wrists) provide the necessary support. The unfolding motion is also frequently used to preset the fingers in anticipation of their becoming part of a larger playing unit. This practice is particularly useful for the subtle voicing of chords.

These ten primary movements encompass the basic elements, positions, and motions used in playing the piano. The student who masters these exercises, notes their kinesthetic sense, and commits their movements and their feel to memory will have a reliable foundation on which to develop a thoroughly competent technique, a technique able to meet the exacting demands of playing. As the movements become second nature, a relatively quick and routine practice of them on a daily basis can serve as a helpful warm-up; they will render the requisite muscle conditioning so the pianist need never be concerned about approaching the instrument less than physically well prepared.

To recapitulate: I started with general posture and then moved on to the larger units of the playing mechanism. I chose this succession because of the comparative ease of learning and memorizing the sensations associated with their movement. Furthermore, the smaller, subtler movements of the hands and fingers are made more difficult when the arms and shoulder girdle function improperly. The upper arms, moving naturally and unconstrainedly through the shoulders and backed by the shoulder girdle, are the prime movers of all good piano technique. They must be trained to move easily in the numerous ways that enable the pianist to deal with the infinitude of possible finger patterns. Not only do they position and systematically support the smaller units, but in slow-moving passages, they commonly initiate each playing movement.

Section 4 Integrative Movements

The ease and joy of pure movement, fostered by learning the primary movements away from the piano with your arms in a relaxed, neutral position, have given you a sense of fluency and expressivity. It is time now to adapt these motions to the requirements of the keyboard in such a way as to preserve this freedom.

The piano requires that the player's arms be pronated and flexed with the fingers pointing downward. The keyboard also mandates a level and laterally straight-line surface against which the fingertips, hands, and arms, whose simplest movements are curved, must operate. The purpose of this section is to carefully blend what we already know kinesthetically about the biomechanics of the core piano-playing movements with the new realities that the instrument presents. There are three integrative areas that I plan to pursue: (1) adapting the shoulder girdle and arms to the keyboard; (2) adapting hand and finger movements to the keyboard; and (3) adapting the entire playing apparatus to integrated cycling at the keyboard.

Integrative Movement 1 Adapting Shoulder and Arm Movements to the Keyboard

The coordinated movements of hands, fingers, arms, and shoulder girdle in Sections 2 and 3 were more easily executed because your arms were usually hanging in their natural position, neither pronated nor flexed. You must now integrate these acquired primary movement skills with the position your body assumes at the piano. If you are not prepared and careful, the obligatory arm pronation and arm flexion can lead to muscular tensions and awkward movements even in the most benign playing posture. So, while making the transition, concentrate on retaining the looseness, freedom, efficiency, and expressivity of movement developed in the first ten primary motions.

I turn to pronation first. Perform PMs 8, 9, and 10 as originally introduced—standing away from the piano with good postural alignment and with your arms hanging loosely. While repeating these exercises, begin to work your shoulder girdle forward little by little, moving your hands around to the front of your legs where your palms face backward (**Fig. 1-19A**). Do each of the several coordinations approximately a dozen times, with your arms at various stages of pronation; determine for yourself the optimal number of repetitions. Return occasionally to the original position—hands near the sides of your legs—to insure that only the direction of the force has changed. The increased pronation of your arms should only minimally alter the kinesthetic sensations you experience and your ability to freely execute these primary movements with your hands and fingers.

Now that you are acquainted with the kinesthetic feelings associated with pronating the arms and hands for the keyboard, I turn to flexion. Seated on a narrow, armless chair with good postural alignment and backed away from the keyboard, perform the exercises of PMs 8, 9, and 10 in pronated position but with arms extended, fingers touching your knees. While executing the movements, flex your elbows little by little until you approximate the angle appropriate for playing **(Fig. 1-19B)**. Note that the shoulder girdle recedes as you flex your elbows. Repeat these several hand and finger coordinations a dozen or so times at various degrees of flexion along your legs to ingrain the adjusted movements, all the while focusing on maintaining the freedom and efficiency of movement acquired in the previous exercises. The movements should feel almost the same as in the earlier exercises despite the new complication of elbow flexion.

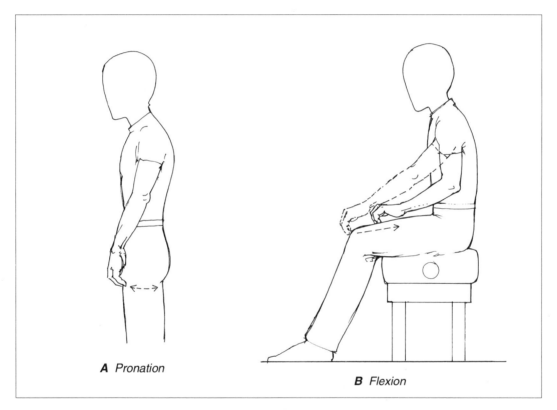

Figure 1-19. The necessary adjustments for assuming the normal playing position (IM 1): (A) pronation; (B) flexion.

Integrative Movement 2 **Adapting Hand and Finger Movements to the Keyboard**

Like the shoulder girdle, the upper arms, and the forearms, the hands and fingers are forced into difficult and awkward positions by the nature of the playing posture at the keyboard. The following exercises aim at integrating the primary movements of the hands and fingers into a new environment. This new environment is the keyboard itself.

Before moving on, review the finger exercises of PM 7.1–7.5, doing them in the air, but now seated with your arms in the normal flexed and pronated playing position with fingers pointing downward. Then proceed to the following exercises.

IM 2.1 This exercise asks you to memorize two contrasting configurations of the hand and fingers in the air as they exist at the beginning and ending of a hypothetical arm rotation at the keyboard. Work calmly and loosely, remembering to be aware of your fingers and hands but without excessive intentness. For the present we will focus on the fingers alone, with the arms remaining still, knuckles level. Memorize the position of the fingers at the pronated extreme of this cycle **(Fig. 1-20A)**: Fingers 1 and 2 are set in the claw position while 5 is set in the palm position; fingers 3 and 4 relax to go where they feel most comfortable. Next, memorize the position at the supinated extreme of the cycle **(Fig. 1-20B)**: Fingers 1 and 2 are set in the palm position with 5 opened out to the extended position; 3 and 4 again relax to go where they are most comfortable. Learn both hand and finger configurations and accustom yourself to oscillating back and forth between them.

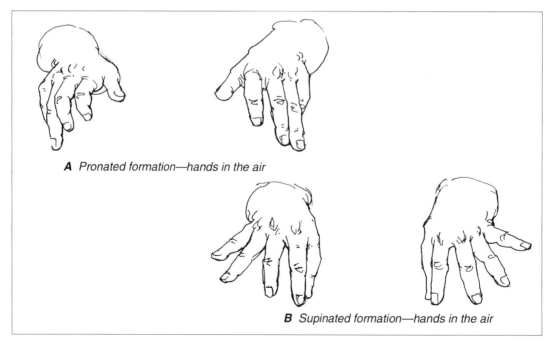

A Pronated formation—hands in the air

B Supinated formation—hands in the air

Figure 1-20. Preparatory finger-positioning practice in the air (IM 2): (A) pronated formation; (B) supinated formation.

IM 2.2 While performing IM 2.1, hands still in the air with fingers pointing downward, blend in the rotary arm cycle mentioned above, adding arm pronation (elbows outward) to **Figure 1-20A** and arm supination (elbows inward) to **Figure 1-20B.** Repeat the composite motion a few dozen times or until the combined pattern is kinesthetically memorized and thoroughly ingrained. Work calmly, concentrating also on keeping the entire playing mechanism as free of tension as possible.

IM 2.3 Perform IM 2.2 seated at the piano with fingers resting loosely and lightly on the level surface of the closed lid. Again, be relaxed and casual, practicing the technique of dissociation so as not to trigger the physical or mental tensions that can inhibit performance. Start with the pronated extreme of the cycle **(Fig. 1-21A)**, change loosely to the supinated extreme of the cycle **(Fig. 1-21B)**, and return: on the thumb sides of the hands, pronated claw fingers 1 and 2 switch to a supinated palm position and back, while on the outside of the hands, pronated palm 5s slide out to the extended position and back. Relaxed fingers roll and slide as necessary, their tips continually touching the flat surface. Flexing (sliding) thumbs can lead movement from position A to position B, flexing (sliding) 5s in the alternate direction. All three joints of fingers 1 and 2 and the knuckles of 5 must be exceptionally mobile as the arch slopes first one way, then the other. Note the interrelation of all moving parts: the moving

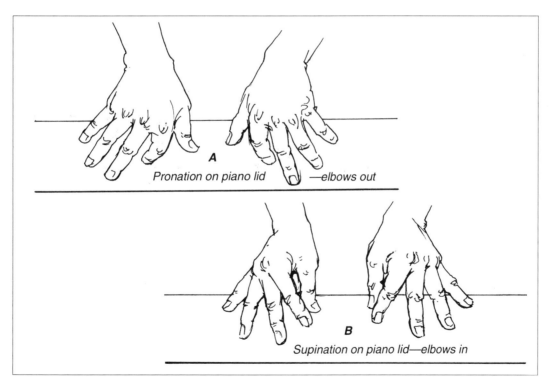

A
Pronation on piano lid —*elbows out*

B
Supination on piano lid—elbows in

Figure 1-21. Integrating arm and finger movements on a flat surface (IM 2): (A) pronated position; (B) supinated position.

shoulder girdle, the laterally hinging upper arms with elbows that barely flex and extend, rotating forearms, continually adapting knuckle, mid-, and terminal joints, and rolling finger pads. Practice this integrated shift several dozen times until it is thoroughly ingrained in a loose, fluid state.

Practiced regularly, the hand calisthenic exercises PMs 7.1–7.5 and IM 2.1–2.3 will provide, like the figure-eight arm gesture of PM 6, a model for the smooth, well-synthesized finger and arm movement required for beautiful playing. These integrated movements provide a flexible basis for balanced, coordinated adaptation to the widely varied and subtly changing demands of the literature. Too often awkwardness in integrating arms and fingers to each other and to the level, double-tiered keyboard surface leads to unintended isometrics, muscular tensions, and stilted playing—performances shaped more by the performer's unconscious physical limitations and mal-coordinations than by his or her intelligent projection of the music's meaning.

Integrative Movement 3 **Adapting the Entire Playing Mechanism to the Keyboard—Arm Cycling**

Piano playing regularly calls for cyclical movements of the arms not only for activating the keys but as a part of the transition from one tone to the next. Thus, the momentum generated to depress the keys is carried over to the preparation and playing of the succeeding keys. A natural pulsation emerges, creating a sense of energy, renewal, and forward progress. These cycles, which take place in either a pulling or pushing direction, simultaneously involve the movement of the shoulder girdle, upper arms, forearms, hands, and fingers. The following exercises are designed to ingrain the effective and efficient marshalling of the entire playing mechanism in producing these repeated cyclical movements.

Seated on a narrow, armless chair with good postural alignment and backed away from the piano, imagine that you are grasping two handles protruding from the two sides of a wheel mounted vertically and perpendicularly from the edge of the keyboard facing you (**Fig. 1-22A**). Turn the wheel with loose fists so that you are pushing it away from you at the top part of the circle, and pulling it towards you at the bottom phase of the cycle. Angle arms somewhat closer to each other at the top, furthest apart starting the upward recoil. The movement is reminiscent of the shoulder-girdle cycles of PMs 2 and 4, except here the forearms are flexed with the upper arms close to the body. Turn the large imaginary wheel several dozen times to exercise and integrate the moving parts of the playing mechanism. Then flatten the circle top and bottom making smaller, faster ellipses (**Fig. 1-22B**). I call this the *pulling arm cycle*. Add speed and pronation to generate "playing" pulsations at the imaginary point of contact on the lower, pulling side of the cycle. Perform cycles of various sizes and speeds, from tiny, quick ones to larger, stretched ones that fill in extended blocks of measured time. Become aware of the fundamental relationship between the speed of repetition and the smallness of the gesture. Cycle size has more to do with how quickly the music can move than does the measured speed of the arm movement itself. The lesson is clear: if you want to play faster, make your movements smaller. The quickest cycles approach a muscular vibration but do not completely achieve it or a straight-line motion.

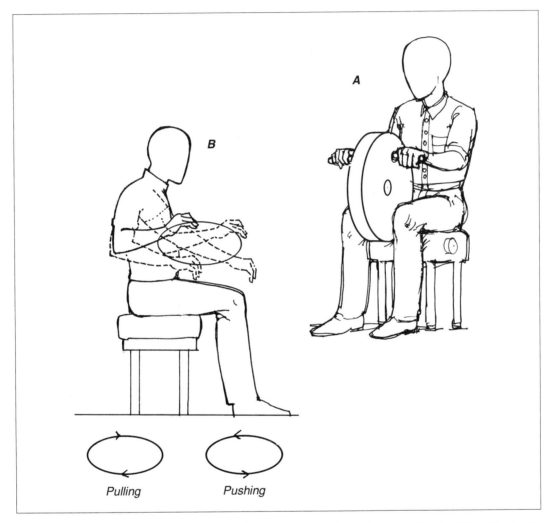

Pulling   Pushing

Figure 1-22. Arm cycling (IM 3): (A) turning an imaginary wheel; (B) elliptical arm cycles.

The *pushing arm cycle* results from turning the imaginary wheel handles in the opposite direction; approach the bottom portion of the cycle with hands (fingers straightened in preparation for the keyboard) moving away from the body. Do several dozen large pushing circles, noting the interrelation of the moving parts, including the shoulder-girdle movement that underlies the action. As before, flatten the circles, decrease their size, and increase the tempo—all while moving. Induce forward "key playing" pulsations by adding speed and pronation at the imaginary contact point. Practice cycling at various speeds and sizes over a period of several weeks, and include those fast and small pushing cycles that approach straight-line motion.

Many useful playing movements are derived from these elliptical models. By integrating shoulder-girdle movement with the smaller units of the playing mechanism, arm cycles help the performer achieve added strength and endurance without any loss of control or subtlety. Also, more than any other single factor, arm cycles in either direction help the performer pace the underlying rhythm of the music and project a sense of forward motion, continuity, and musical line.

Section 5 **Movements Shaped by the Piano**

It is impossible to properly use the playing mechanism, which in the previous exercises we have honed to a point of efficient, musically intelligent movement, unless it is correctly addressed to the keyboard. In short, you must position your body at the keyboard with the same care and attention that you give to refining the movements of the playing mechanism itself.

This section deals with two additional areas of consequence which must be taken into account. They are (1) the player's physical and psychological relationship to the topography of the keyboard; and (2) the player's articulation with the pedals leading to their efficient, musically imaginative use.

5 A **Posture at the Keyboard**

Position and posture before the keyboard, where and how you sit, require careful consideration and consistent application, for they are the foundation on which all playing movement rests. Since no two people have identical physical proportions, you must arrive at the best positioning for yourself.

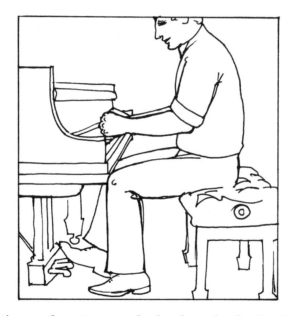

Figure 1-23. Position and posture at the keyboard—the fundamental technique.

Experiment as follows, using an adjustable, solid, hard-surfaced stool or bench without arms, to discover your unique *central position*. Sit with good postural alignment and your body centered before middle D, occupying one-half to two-thirds of the width of the sitting surface **(Fig. 1-23)**. Sitting in this manner provides efficient weight distribution while also providing sufficient body support and freedom for pedaling. Once centered, aim to simultaneously realize the remaining positional relationships:

1. Your bench or stool must be at a height so that when your body is comfortably poised—that is, when your spine and neck are lengthened, and your body is tilted slightly forward of vertical with the upper arms near and parallel to your body—your flexed but nonpronated forearms create a horizontal line between the bottoms of the keys and your elbows.

2. Your bench or stool must allow you to sit close enough to the keyboard so that with your upper arms comfortably vertical your right fist presses the cluster C-D-E one octave above middle D while your left fist presses the cluster C-D-E one octave below middle D. The fifth finger knuckles of both hands should just touch the white area of the keyboard.

Integrate these two dimensions of height and proximity to the keyboard by pronating the hands to the normal playing position: elbows drift slightly forward and outward. Play in this position for 15–20 minutes making any adjustments you deem necessary. Experiment an additional 15–20 minutes. Finally, consciously and decisively choose the central position that feels best and stay with it. A well-established central position not only speeds habit formation and promotes accuracy, but it also frees the player's mind to focus on ways to make his or her playing movements more musically responsive.

Establishing a healthful and natural posture at the outset is critical because the many hours devoted to practice will only prove harmful if your back slumps, your head hangs, or your shoulders hunch. Your sitting torso-neck-head alignment must replicate your standing posture, with the head balanced forward and upward, the spine elongated, and the shoulders released outward to gravity. This position stabilizes the spinal column by minimizing and balancing the muscular effort needed to maintain your equilibrium. By contrast, a sagging posture hinging at the waist inhibits breathing, triggers an unhealthy rigidity of opposing trunk muscles to keep from sagging further, and blocks the free movement of the shoulders and arms. You must arrive at a correct position for yourself and stay with it.

Sitting spinal extension is encouraged by relaxing the muscles of your tongue, jaw, neck, chest, and lower back. Simultaneously contract your lower abdominal muscles, thus widening your lower back and aligning the lower area of the torso properly. Sit directly (think "stand") on your "sit-bones," the two bony prominences at the bottom of your pelvis. By so doing you will almost instinctively sense the poised unity and verticality of your entire upper body. From this centered, neutral position, tilt forward slightly hinging at the hips to throw a good deal of body weight forward on your thighs. So positioned your knees can drift apart adding to a feeling of body relaxation and stability: the greater resistance felt by your legs against the bench or stool will tell you that your upper body is properly placed to support and utilize the playing mechanism most effectively.

Now place the ball, not your toes, of your right foot on the damper pedal, the heel firmly planted on the floor. The left foot, rarely needed for the *una corda* or sostenuto pedal, is typically placed diagonally outward on the floor, poised to provide support or counterweight to the bodily movements involved in playing. Absolutely avoid any hamstring pull that slides your feet backward or tips the bench forward.

Your body, now centered in balanced equilibrium, fulfills two necessary functions:

1. It can move easily and gracefully to express musical line and continuity.
2. It effectively positions and supports the finely tuned playing actions of the shoulder girdle, arms, hands, and fingers.

The torso-neck-head unit should move as one. Movement toward and away from the piano is made hinging at the hips, never at the waist. Lateral movement is done by swaying right or left—always maintaining the postural alignment of the central seated position.

Play a flowing musical line making slow, elliptical circles with your shoulders, and note the changes that occur in weight distribution, muscle support, and balance **(Fig. 1-24)**. Note that as you move toward the farthest point of each circle you must alternately elongate (relax) the upper side of your middle trunk to keep your hip from raising off the chair. The legs also play their part. Circle a dozen times to accustom yourself to the gentle sway and to moving the torso-neck-head unit without losing equilibrium.

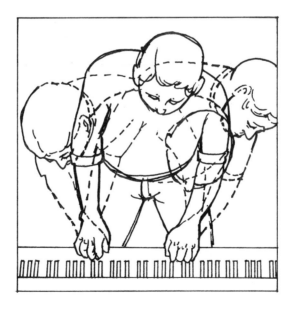

Figure 1-24. Body movement flowing with the musical line.

Next, we turn to those movements useful for positioning the hands along the full length of the keyboard. Only three movements are needed to readily and effectively reach the extreme ends of the keyboard.

The one involving the simplest movement is interestingly enough the one required to reach the extreme ends simultaneously. To do so simply bend farther forward from the hips towards the keyboard, thereby extending the arms' lateral reach to the outside.

The second movement, which allows you to position both hands to the extreme right, requires that you sway to the right on the right hip while lengthening (relaxing) your left side. Simultaneously twist the torso slightly to the left to align your hands with the fallboard by pulling your left knee and lower leg back. Slide your left foot as far left as needed to provide a counter-weight to the off-center position of the upper body (**Fig. 1-25**).

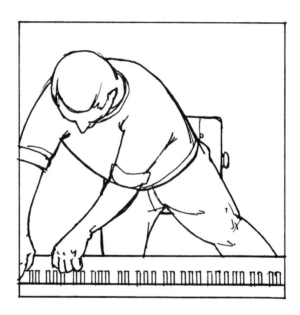

Figure 1-25. Body movement reaching extreme right. Note the counter-balancing left leg.

The third movement allows you to extend both hands to the extreme left. It requires that you sway to the left on the left hip while extending (relaxing) your right side. Simultaneously slide your left foot to the left to provide added support and twist your body slightly to the right to align your hands with the fallboard by pulling your right knee back. Remember to keep your head up, the spine lengthened, and the shoulder girdle released to the outside at all times.

Take the time to memorize the kinesthetic feelings of these movements away from your central position. You should experiment with these movements while also playing, but for the time being pay no attention to the quality of your playing, only to the bodily sensations you experience. The body must maintain its equilibrium without any recourse to the playing apparatus, which is to say that your shoulder girdle, arms, hands, and fingers never become supports for your trunk; you never lean on the piano with your hands to hold the body up. Rather the opposite must happen, these playing members are positioned and stabilized by your torso and legs even as your torso moves to express musical continuity. Thus relieved of all balancing obligations, the playing apparatus remains free to operate the keyboard in the most effective, efficient, and musically intelligent way. Bodily awkwardness, which is far too often evident even among accomplished players, typically leads to distortions of rhythm and tone.

5 B The Shape of and Relations Within the Keyboard

Make a point of watching several skilled sight readers and chamber music players to note how seldom they establish eye contact with the keyboard, and how steadily they focus their gaze on the printed score before them. In so doing they demonstrate what many student musicians feel is an uncanny awareness of where to place their hands, a sixth sense of the arrangement of the keys in space. This topographical knowledge is a basic building block in constructing a musically intelligent technique. For most performers, direct, systematic training is the best way to gain this topographical proficiency. As you work to develop this, you will find yourself becoming increasingly well-oriented and comfortable, both spatially and kinesthetically, with the instrument, and hence able to play with greater ease and freedom.

Look afresh at the narrow plateau of the keyboard stretching laterally as wide as the average person's reach. It clearly consists of two tiers of levers or keys; the black ones are higher, shorter, and narrower than the white ones which are lower, longer and, at their near ends, wider. Though it all looks quite orderly and thought-out, the structure bears little obvious relation to the logic of music. But now, focus on the repeating pattern of octaves contained within the keyboard, each octave consisting of five black and seven white keys. This octave duplication in various registers is fundamental to both the keyboard and musical structure, and should therefore be systematically incorporated in all your reasoning about music, including your analyzing, learning, and fingering procedures.

Now look again at the keyboard to see another fundamental pattern—a pattern that presents some genuine difficulties. The double-tiered levers used to produce the tones are asymmetrically placed in the octave; the higher black keys are in two groups—one of two keys, the other of three. As a consequence, semitone spacing is only visually consistent in the black-key area of the keyboard, where all keys, black and white, high and low, are roughly of the same narrow width. But in the lower tier, the white keys, which for the most part represent whole steps, can also at times indicate semitones; the width of the levers in either case is the same. This divergence of physical proportion from musical proportion, compounded by the ever-changing height level adjustments required of the fingers, can bewilder a player. These anomalies complicate ordinary chromatic transpositions. Moving a major triad typically fingered 1-3-5, chromatically, for example, forces the player to repeatedly adjust the shape of the hand to compensate for the spatial irregularities of the keyboard, irregularities that prompt some players to change fingering even though dealing with identical musical shapes. Yet the ability to render such chromatic transposition with consistent fingering is an essential part of the sophistication needed to play with musical insight, and so must be mastered notwithstanding the visual, intellectual, and physical difficulties connected with the layout of the keyboard.

Begin the process of orienting yourself to the arrangement of the keyboard by centering yourself before the piano: center yourself physically by identifying middle D, not middle C, as the keyboard's spatial center; center yourself psychologically by conceiving of lateral movement as proceeding outward from, or inward to, this center. For the present, forego concepts like right and left, up and down, or sideways, and substitute notions that encourage center-outward thinking. Pianists function quite comfortably in this bilaterally symmetrical mode; the player's body remains centered in front of middle D in the mirrored middle of the keyboard as both sides of the body relate to that center in terms of balanced, contrary movement. So assume your central position in front of middle D and proceed.

Become skilled first in octave transposition: with your right hand transpose single notes, chords, and melodic motives to the three complete octave registers bounded by D on the right-hand side of the piano. Maintain identical fingering as you jump from register to register. Practice the mirror image of this octave transposition procedure with your left hand, skipping around the three complete octaves bounded by D on the left-hand side of the piano. When you are ready, expand the range of each of your hands, one hand at a time, crossing over to cover all six octaves. Do these exercises for 10–15 minutes a day until they become second nature and you have physically and intellectually internalized the feeling of the octave patterning.

With octave transposition under control, turn to experiencing the mirrored topographical relationships associated with contrary motion centered on middle D. Play a slow legato contrary chromatic scale using the traditional 1-(2)-3 fingering: Start with both thumbs on middle D touching in the gray area, sound the black keys to either side with third fingers, and continue outward. Play all black keys with third fingers, single whites with thumbs, and double whites using fingers 1 and 2. Progress in contrary motion for three full octaves, both arms together, and return using identical fingering. Play softly, with minimal movement and tension, and with the longer fingers somewhat extended. Sense the weight of each key you play and realize from the start that the looser and softer you play, the quicker the topographical learning takes place. This is true because the more malleable your hands and fingers remain, the quicker they can sense and react to the shapes encountered. Third fingers touch their black keys reaching out towards the fallboard, and second fingers play their white keys well within the black key area, squeezing sideways against the nearby black key. Notice that contrary chromatic scales begun on middle D yield mirror-image relationships with identical physical movements for both hands.

Now play a four-octave parallel D-major scale with hands one octave apart, beginning on Ds at the bass end of the piano. Notice that the two sides of your body must perform vastly differing coordinations simultaneously. Despite the theoretical simplicity of a doubled, single line between the hands, from the physical point of view of the player, the coordinative task is infinitely more difficult and complicated than that of the previous contrary chromatic scale.

This is a prime example of the confusion that can arise by focusing on technique as a series of musical patterns rather than coming to grips with the body mechanics of the player. Furthermore, parallel movement tends to push the body off-center, requiring compensating adjustments by the legs and torso. These, then, are my reasons for establishing center-outward thinking and contrary, bilateral movement as the fundamental components of keyboard orientation and technical development. Scales obviously have a place in technical development, and they can always be practiced one hand at a time; but in my view scales are not the best vehicle for establishing the primary mental and physical orientation to the instrument.

The following series of exercises not only center you at the keyboard, but also help you relate its irregular shape to the symmetrical, mirrored movement of your arms, hands, and fingers. Consistently centering yourself will automatically improve your lateral hand and finger accuracy as your mind begins to comprehend the inherent order of the keyboard that results from middle D, mirror-image, contrary movement reasoning. The mind perceives this new orientation as an important unifying and indeed simplifying element.

Little by little as you practice these exercises there develops what I call a *hand vocabulary*. This term implies a consistent choice of fingering that relates not so much to the layout of black and white keys, but to the intervalic structure of the tones. A meaningful finger-interval bonding emerges. For example, while transposing a given musical shape, say the aforementioned triad fingered 1-3-5, the original fingering of that triad remains constant so long as the intervals of the triad are unaltered. Though the shape of the hand may change slightly with particular fingers sometimes high or low (including thumbs on black keys), the significant point is that the player learns to adjust a constant fingering to the irregular spatial relationships of the keyboard. The intervalic distances of the tones become consequentially tied to certain hand-finger configurations which can be regularly applied throughout a given passage or an entire composition. To successfully apply hand-vocabulary logic, a player must feel thoroughly comfortable playing near the fallboard in the black area of the keyboard, using thumbs on black keys, playing white notes with longer fingers between black keys, and negotiating the varying heights of the two-tier system.

Hand-vocabulary thinking requires studying and organizing the repetitive shapes of a musical composition, and systematically applying interval-fingering equivalencies. Doing this leads to the most profound reward of the process. As a given fingering pattern defines the possibilities for arm move-ment, then the regularity of the fingering sets the arms free to choreograph the repetitive musical shapes in a consistent, straightforward manner. In time, you will discover the great extent to which the arms hold the secrets to power, facility, pacing, and tonal control in beautiful piano playing. But this cannot happen unless you establish the knowledgeable, consistent, musically-oriented fingering that allows the arms to be used to their full potential.

Keeping this goal in mind, resume the training to reorient your approach to that of center-outward thinking. Repeat the contrary chromatic scale from middle D to find the coincident Ds and G♯s. These coincident tones form equidistant, half-octave, tritone (three whole steps) intervals along the keyboard. They can be labeled and used as signposts that show the distance in both directions from middle D—via half-octave G♯s—to three-octave Ds. Six octaves separate the hands when playing three-octave Ds (**Fig. 1-26**).

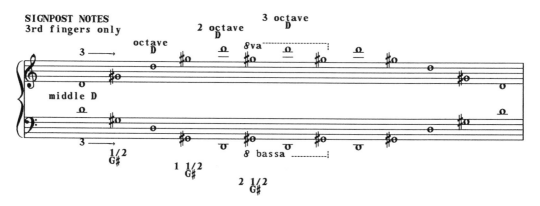

Figure 1-26. Middle D with signpost notes—black area contrary motion arm practice for the purpose of psychologically and physically centering yourself at the keyboard.

Perform the notes in **Figure 1-26** hands together and with straightened third fingers, whose pads (not tips) touch near the fallboard. Form your hands and fingers so that a gradual, elongated arc is inscribed from the fingernails through the joints of the fingers to high wrists. The arrangement is similar to the one naturally formed by letting your hands hang loosely from wrists poised in the normal playing position. Sound the notes using a prepared (fingers beginning on the keys) arm-push stroke; this is the washboard stroke described in PM 5. Play each pair of notes softly several times, stroking your upper arms gently forward with minimal movement and tension, and with a sense of musical line. The looser your hands and fingers, the more readily they can sense and react to the weight of the keys and to the irregularities of key height. Experience with each key both its resistance and the forward friction of the finger pads against the key surfaces. Make smooth tritone shifts. Play blacks and whites identically; push the white Ds forward close to the fallboard between their neighboring blacks. Begin the exercise in full view, but work to develop so profound a kinesthetic feel for the lateral distances that you can locate the signpost notes without looking.

Fill in the tritone spaces as shown in **Figure 1-27**. The purpose of this exercise is to accustom you to playing single-fingered, contrary chromatic scales with your arms. Using the same fingers, placement, and touch parameters as in the previous exercise, play as though "seeing" with relaxed fingers. Feel your way along the keyboard—the way blind people track their fingers along a corridor wall to discover door openings and turnings—guided by the sides and tops of the keys. Height adjustments for the keys are identical for both arms. When playing whites with blacks to only one side, squeeze diagonally against those blacks for added security. Avoid sagging arms; that is, do not sound white keys by sliding down from their neighboring blacks. All keys, white and black, are played identically, sliding forward near the fallboard. Move through these relatively cramped quarters without looking and with an increasing awareness of the outlines of the mirrored shapes. Touch the keys with your finger pads, and with closed eyes picture the physical pattern of the keyboard in your mind's eye.

Figure 1-27. **Tritone spaces filled in chromatically. Arms experience the two-tier system in the black area of the keyboard.**

The exercise pattern in **Figure 1-28** alternates octave and chromatic motion with the third fingers. The purpose here is to learn to make accurate contrary octave shifts of the arms, while using the same fingers, positioning, and touch coordination of the previous two exercises. The proper shoulder-girdle and upper-arm movements to be employed are described in PM 6. Make smooth, balanced shifts with upper arms leading the lateral movement. If necessary, you may practice one arm at a time to begin with, but play hands together as soon as possible.

Figure 1-28. Alternating contrary octave and chromatic motion—further centering practice.

To help with the precision of the "cross-eyed" contrary shifts, focus on the mirror-image aspect of the black key groupings. Remembering that middle D is the center for the entire series serves to root you in the center of the piano in your chosen central position. When this and the two previous exercises feel completely comfortable using third fingers (the middle of the hand), experiment with using paired second, then paired fourth fingers as well.

It is time now to concentrate on the relationships within the octave. A useful way to simplify the irregularities of the black key patterning is to project two contrasting areas of the octave: a predominantly black one and a predominantly white one. Do this by establishing two sets of five adjacent keys, each series of keys centered around a signpost key **(Fig. 1-29)**.

Notice how G♯ centers the group of three blacks that are upper tier, black, and *do-re-mi* in F♯ major. Similarly, D centers a group of three white keys that are lower tier, white, and *do-re-mi* in C major. The groups, opposite in character, have a tritone relationship that can be exploited for further topographical training.

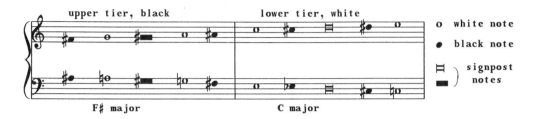

Figure 1-29. The high and low signpost centers—organization within the octave.

Play the chord clusters in **Figure 1-30** entirely in the black area near the fallboard, through the full three-octave contrary motion range of the original signpost exercise pattern **(Fig. 1-26)**. The third fingers are to be placed on the signpost Ds and G♯s. The circled finger numbers in **Figure 1-30** signify which fingers are to be used on the primary notes. Practice each of the given exercises (A and B) at least a half-dozen times, until you can execute the shifts easily and unerringly, without looking at the keyboard. Habituate your mind and hands to experience the two-tiered, black-white key system as high and low, not as far and near. This important adjustment comes about quite naturally since all fingers are touching in the black area. Maintain your focus on lateral accuracy and on adjusting the relative height at which each finger must be placed to accurately mold to the next landing. These height adjustments are made in midair by fingers acting individually and independently, with the knuckle lines of the hands maintained substantially parallel to both the keyboard and fallboard, and with the arms and the wrists quiet. The essence of keyboard facility lies in the ability to anticipate the lateral arm shifts and vertical finger molds with pinpoint precision.

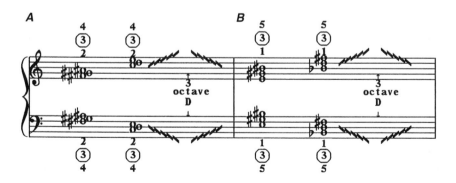

Figure 1-30. Signpost note clusters—training the fingers to the two-tier system.

The pattern in **Figure 1-31A** is made up of the chromatic, octave, and tritone movements, all commonly encountered in music, but in an abbreviated form. Practice it to develop facility in transposing two- and three-note hand-vocabulary units. Before moving on, thoroughly learn the basic sequence pattern, once again using straightened third fingers played near the fallboard with small, gentle, washboard strokes.

Now play Figure **1-31B**, which is identical to the pattern in **Figure 1-31A**, in contrary thirds with fingers 3 and 5. Note that the third fingers (represented in the figure by the circled number 3s) play the primary note of the template pattern; fifth fingers follow along at their set distance of a major third. Touch fingers near the fallboard well into the black area of the keyboard. Adjust finger heights independently, that is, with finger action alone, avoiding unnecessary in/out or angling movements of the arms. Play by pushing lightly forward, finger pads touching before each stroke, with little tension or movement, and with fingers forming a comfortably extended position. Continue to "see" with the pads and sides of your fingers.

A

B

Figure 1-31. Basic template practice model which includes chromatic, octave, and tritone transposition: (A) the primary notes of the exercise pattern; (B) pattern with thirds added to the outside.

Repeat the exercise with fingers 2 and 4, then with fingers 1 and 3. Again place the circled finger number on the primary tone of the exercise pattern. Refer to the series of "starting intervals" in **Figure 1-32**, taking each set of the indicated fingerings through the entire pattern established in **Figure 1-31A**. You may certainly enlarge the pattern for additional practice. Repeat each finger set several times to accustom your fingers to shifting independently and to maintaining the given intervalic distances. Again sound the tones by stroking gently forward with straightened fingers, playing softly, with minimal tension and motion, and with a sense of musical line.

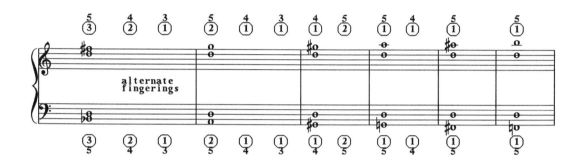

Figure 1-32. Two-note hand-vocabulary shapes to be applied to the practice model—"starting intervals."

Approach the three-note chords of **Figure 1-33** similarly. After practicing one hand at a time, use both hands together to take each pair of chords through all the notes of the basic drill pattern established in **Figure 1-31A**. Again, play softly with minimal tension and movement. Practice each of the option fingerings until they can be performed with both hands together comfortably, unerringly, and with a sense of musical line.

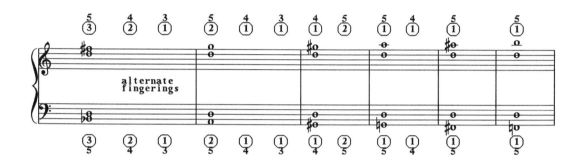

Fingering applies to both hands.

Figure 1-33. Three-note hand-vocabulary shapes to be applied to the practice model—"starting positions."

We have been through a process of molding your mind, arms, hands, and fingers to the topography of the keyboard from the vantage point of your central position. Developing a comfortable and routine proficiency in hand-vocabulary orientation and its mirrored-movement transposition contributes profoundly to an instinctual understanding of keyboard topography as well as to genuine technical sophistication. The easy management of the keyboard grows as your fingers become habituated to using its entire depth and to handling the two-tier relationship of the keys. Your arms gain lateral accuracy as you remain centered at the keyboard. This growing proficiency frees you to give your attention to the elements found within the musical score, to intervalic relationships, melodic shapes, and rhythmic organization—all of which form the basis for intelligent performance. These musical components can be consistently and logically ordered and fingered, and then applied to the piano with a newfound versatility and latitude. Your mind, arms, hands, and fingers become free to choreograph the shapes and contours you find in the music rather than remaining tied in a superficial relationship to an arbitrary keyboard design. This will significantly add to your playing a genuine sense of freedom, artistic meaning, and expression.

5 C **The Pedals**

The tonal characteristics of the piano are greatly enhanced by its ability to enrich and sustain the tones produced. This function is performed by the damper pedal, which not only moderates the percussiveness of tone production but permits the player to hold, accumulate, or connect pitches well beyond what the fingers alone can do. These inflections and transformations of tonal quality are unique to the instrument, allowing it to sing in ways no other instrument can. One quickly realizes how central pedaled sonorities are to the quality of piano sound when hearing what is lost, particularly in idiomatic piano works like those of Chopin or Debussy, in transcriptions of piano works to other instruments or combinations of instruments.

When the damper pedal is not engaged, the keys control the felt dampers of their respective strings so that when a key is struck the tone sounds until it is released. Engagement of the damper pedal raises the entire bank of felt dampers, thus overriding the control of an individual key's damper and sustaining the tone even when the key is released, until the pedal is released. Furthermore, because undamped strings are free to vibrate sympathetically with activated strings, the overall resonance of the instrument is markedly enriched when the pedal is engaged.

It is time now to incorporate the pedals into your central position. Place the ball of your foot, not just the toe, securely on the pedal, heel touching the floor (**Fig. 1-34**). The movement to depress the pedal is made by the ankle, but since the heel is hinged to the floor the player experiences associated movement in both the knee and hip joints. The unfolding leg produces forward (avoid pulling) friction on the pedal surface.

Figure 1-34. Damper pedal action—the exaggerated release.

Though the pedal is occasionally engaged simultaneously with the depression of a key or keys by the finger(s) to enrich sonority, its primary function is to sustain and connect tones. To effect this binding of tones in a musically intelligent way, a legato or syncopated pedal must be employed and it must be executed with precision, speed, and subtlety. The most important aspect of sensitive legato pedaling is in knowing when to release the pedal; sounds accumulated by virtue of engaging the pedal must be precisely damped so they are musically integrated with the succeeding sounds.

The objective of this section is to provide you with the physical and intellectual means of using the pedals efficiently, effectively, and in a musically imaginative way. It will be necessary to repeat these exercises over an extended period of time so that the movements become thoroughly instinctive, agile, and most important, wedded to your concentrated listening.

Depress the pedal slowly, listening for a tantalizing kind of aliveness within the instrument. Then, keeping your heel securely hinged to the floor, snap your foot back as far and fast as possible, noticing how high your knee is raised. Snap it so sharply that the returning dampers generate a thud. Hold your toe high, well above the pedal, and attend to the dead silence that ensues. Repeat these exaggerated movements rhythmically, matching ONE to the thud of the pedal release, TWO to the following calm pedal depression. Note how the sharp release is clearly separated from the subsequent depression.

Next play a one-finger (any finger) scale in the rhythms indicated in **Figure 1-35A**, a quarter to MM 100. The upper arrows pointing downward call for depressing the key while those pointing upward call for releasing the key. The lower diagonally descending lines call for depressing the pedal while those pointing upward call for a quick release. The key is depressed and held with the finger until the pedal is re-engaged, while the playing of the next note must be synchronized with the thud of the exaggerated pedal release.

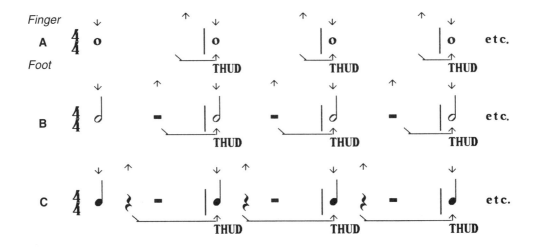

Figure 1-35. Legato pedal exercise pattern.

Repeat the three exercises in **Figure 1-35** until you can accurately connect the notes in the varied rhythmic patterns, all the while developing ankle mobility and the extremely critical integration of hand, foot, and ear. Enlarge your practice of single-finger scales to include skips, then random chords jumping around, all carefully and cleanly connected with the damper pedal. Practice each hand separately and both hands together. These drills are designed to develop basic legato pedal instincts. All three exercises encourage habits which involve careful listening, exact timing, deftness of movement, and absolute separation of strokes. Practice these exercises until the contrary motion between finger and foot becomes second nature.

When you have the three parts of **Figure 1-35** well in hand at the slow tempo suggested above, then turn to the even-cycled exercise **(Fig. 1-35B)**. Increase speed from ♩ = MM 100 to MM 200 over a period of several days. At some point in increasing speed you will find that you must abandon the exaggerated pedal release, but even so, do not abandon the crispness of the release movement.

Continue your practice with the exercise in Figure 1-35B, using **o** = MM 100. Boost speed gradually until you have time to neither depress the pedal nor lift your foot completely. By listening carefully you can discover the engagement point of the pedal mechanism—the precise location, surrounded by free play movement—where the dampers actually leave the strings. This point will vary from instrument to instrument. Fast, tiny movements at the engagement point create a vibrato pedal, a technique useful for very fast passages requiring a sustained, pedaled sonority while calling for relative tonal clarity and differentiation.

When the basic legato pedaling motion becomes thoroughly ingrained, it is time to turn to more subtle applications. Realize immediately that the damper pedal is not simply a toggle switch with two extreme positions, but rather a device with which to control resonance by varying the speed, timing, and degree of depression. Thus you can release the pedal early, to articulate between sonorities; or late, to produce a merging legato. You can half-release to extinguish only part of the old sonority before adding a new one. You can create contrast by pedaling some sonorities while not pedaling others, an effect valuable in performing music of the classical period. You can depress the pedal before activating the key(s) to augment sympathetic vibrations, or maximize crescendos by letting sounds accumulate over extended periods of time. You can depress the pedal only a portion of its full movement to ration the amount of sonority and resonance accumulated. You can vary tonal decay from a sharp, accented release to a slow, vibrato fading away. You can simulate *fp* on sustained notes and exploit sympathetic vibrations to create overtones. All these and other possibilities are open to you after mastering the legato pedal.

Since the damper pedal is so critical an element in the functional and artistic makeup of the instrument it behooves the player to pay scrupulous attention to its use, to listen extremely carefully, and to habituate the foot, mind, and ear to creatively explore the manifold number of musical opportunities it opens. Continually experiment to discover how sonorities variously pedaled can increase the range and beauty of your playing. Always keep in mind that the manner and amount of pedaling you apply in each instance must vary with the particular instrument, the room or hall, and even the size of the audience. Pedaling, like other physical factors in technique, is only roughly or approximately preset—you must continually listen to the actual sounds you bring to life at the moment of creation and be prepared to adjust your pedal movements accordingly. Ride the pedal to obtain just that degree of sustaining, enriching, and overlapping of sound required to project your ideal concept and meaning of the music, not unlike the way string players will vary the speed and width of their vibrato to express subtleties of phrasing or mood. At this stage, pedaling becomes an intuitive, unconscious extension of inner hearing and artistic expression, objectives unattainable without a thorough understanding and complete physical control of the damper pedal.

The other two pedals require no special dexterity and they are used relatively rarely. The left, *una corda* or soft pedal shifts the playing action to the right just enough for the hammers to hit the strings on a softer part of the felt or in the case of those higher tones on the modern piano strung with three strings, the hammers hit only two strings while the third string vibrates sympathetically. A contrasting, slightly muffled tone color is created. Keep in mind that using the *una corda* is not primarily a substitute for the inability to play softly with fingers alone. Much like a harpsichord's lute stop or a violin's mute, the use of the soft pedal should largely be confined to changing tone color in blocked, sectional, and terraced contrasts.

The sostenuto or middle pedal is the least used of the three, though recently composers have exploited its possibilities. When depressed it engages only those dampers that are already raised by previously depressed and held keys. These raised dampers are caught by the sostenuto pedal and will remain off their strings until the sostenuto pedal is released. All other keys function normally and can be played with or without damper pedal in the usual manner. So long as the sostenuto pedal is engaged before the damper and after the specified keys have been depressed, it will override the damper pedal's control of those dampers it holds. Do not, however, depress the sostenuto pedal after the damper pedal is engaged, for it will then catch and hold the complete bank of dampers, and any specialized sostenuto pedal effects will be lost.

The sostenuto pedal is sometimes used to sustain a low, bass note below changing, cleanly pedaled harmonies. Although most piano music was composed for instruments lacking this device, you nonetheless should feel free to employ it whenever it can enhance an artistic effect. Carefully preplan its use; it is not a pedal for spur-of-the-moment "inspiration."

Section 6 **Summary**

The exercises and instructions of Part One established the requisite mental, physical, and emotional underpinnings for productive technical development. Working methods and attitudes, practice procedures, postural concerns, habit formation, and velocity training were interwoven with the presentation of the ten primary movements. These core movements, isolated from each other and from their normal application at the piano, allowed you to focus completely on the biomechanics of your own movement and to systematically develop physically efficient, well-coordinated movement patterns. At the same time you came to appreciate the potential that pure movement has for emotional expression.

The primary movements, for the most part, maintained the arms in their most neutral, relaxed position and emphasized the equal development of both sides of the body. Stressing at first correct postural alignment, five additional basic arm and shoulder-girdle exercises were presented whose goal was to develop freedom and efficiency of movement, in all directions, at the shoulders, and to integrate these larger movement elements with the elbows and forearms.

The final four primary movements were devoted to hands and fingers. A theoretical scheme was introduced that accounts for most hand and finger movement: this included the three primary hand positions (extended, palm, and claw positions) and the two basic finger coordinations (pulling and unfolding fingers) that tie the hand positions together. The importance of scooping hands, something often overlooked, preceded the exercises devoted to mastering the pulling and unfolding finger coordinations. The emphasis continued on equalizing the development of both sides of the body.

The three integrative movement patterns combined separate movement elements and adopted them for use at the piano. The final sections of Part One served to orient you to and center you at the instrument itself. These sections included ideas and exercises that helped you to address the piano, helped you to comprehend and relate to the shape and contours of its keyboard, and which guided you to a productive use of the pedal, that very special pianistic device.

Part One introduced the basic terminology and central biomechanics of pianistic movement, and covered many of the mental and procedural elements that support intelligent technical development. Part Two will relate what you have learned so far to live sound at the piano.

Part Two **Applied Movements**

Section 7   **Introduction**

Part One introduced the primary movements of piano playing away from the piano in a centered, relaxed, and expanded mode, stressing the efficiency, balance, and expressiveness of pure movement. Postural alignment, habit formation, gesture continuity, velocity training, and instrumental considerations were also addressed. The material was presented with a double purpose: to provide students with a general overview of the body mechanics involved in piano playing; and to increase their powers of self-observation and awareness, both visual and kinesthetic. Pianists should try to become so keenly aware of the inner sensations of their playing movement as to render themselves substantially more injury-proof at the instrument.

Dangers exist for committed pianists who push the body too far. These dangers are caused not only by inefficient physical movements, but also by the sheer intensity of the musical experience and the zeal to excel, both of which may be superimposed on the generalized tension and stress of busy lives and performance deadlines. Students' best deterrent to pushing too far is continuing alertness to their own bodies, understanding the principles of body efficiency and, at the same time, its limitations. Serious performers must focus on the ongoing physical processes, even as they set their sights on ultimate musical or career enhancing ends, and they must assiduously apply what they have learned about practice routines, habit formation, and the importance of coolly pacing their work.

Part Two, Applied Movements, begins the process of applying the fundamental movements of Part One to the keyboard to create sound and musical shape, while Part Three, Synthesized Movement, addresses more sophisticated technical material relating to the interaction of fingers with hands and arms. These latter two parts present instructions and exercises that progressively point performers towards a balanced and flexible technique, one that will support and encourage continuing musical and pianistic growth. By the end of the process, a large variety of movement choices will have been presented. Some coordinations will feel particularly natural, or perhaps create especially pleasing sounds, and thus become staples in one's approach to the instrument; other coordinations will be used only sparingly for special musical effects. A wealth of movement choice is developed to be held in reserve, ready to be tapped in performance, often subconsciously, to do the performer's musical bidding. The expertise is also developed to help players confront, analyze, and resolve the technical problems that arise in the literature they are studying.

Part Two subdivides the initial application of the fundamental movements to the keyboard into five major areas of the playing apparatus, each named after the portion of the mechanism that seems to be primary. The progression from larger to smaller playing elements, followed in Part One, is retained in Part Two. The five substantive areas, which comprise Sections 8 through 12 of Part Two, are as follows:

1. Upper arm and shoulder-girdle coordinations with pushing, pulling, and cycling in the shoulder.
2. Forearm coordinations with elbow movement.
3. Hand coordinations with wrist movement.
4. Thumb coordinations with palm-knuckle movement.
5. Finger coordinations with hand-knuckle movement.

At the piano, individual differences become more important as body size and proportion, hand size and shape, previous training and experience, and motivation vary from person to person. None of these is gender-specific; the physical characteristics of men and women, in so far as the piano is concerned, overlap to a remarkable degree. Furthermore, even physical strength at the piano derives largely from coordinated movement and is not primarily dependent upon general physical robustness.

In the following exercises I have sought to minimize those differences by focusing the presentation on the kinds of movement mechanics that pertain to anyone, even though variously sized and shaped hands might well look different when performing identical coordinations. The technique presented here is concerned primarily with the movements the player makes, their kinesthetic feelings, and how the various parts of the playing mechanism relate to each other and to the keyboard. Students should feel free to proceed at a comfortable rate, determining for themselves what to study at a given time, and when to move on. Finally, keep in mind that players can always accommodate the exercises to fit their own body proportions, and still profit from the ideas and systematic training offered in the book.

Unless otherwise specified, the exercises that follow are to be performed hands together in contrary motion. Proceed as before—reviewing earlier material, working thoughtfully in repeated short sessions and following generally in order. Feel free, however, to do some jumping around. You can certainly work several sections simultaneously so long as you maintain the order within each section; but do substantially complete Part Two before embarking on Part Three. Notwithstanding the need for a certain developmental evolution, I recommend working in those sections that speak most directly to your present needs, filling in previous material as required. More and more you should take responsibility for the direction and pace of your technical work, for this encourages its growth. Once you feel comfortable with a new movement, apply it to your work in the literature, and explore other musical examples that fit the pattern. I have supplied a few excerpts of varying difficulty for additional practice. Try all of them, for even those examples played below tempo can demonstrate how the movements under discussion relate to significant musical works. This is not to say that these examples might not also be approached using somewhat different movements; a final technical choice would depend upon your considered musical conception and on your inner hearing of the passage.

Section 8 Upper Arms and Shoulder Girdle

Sit at the piano in your centered position, taking time to set a good postural alignment. Review the pulling and pushing arm cycles of IM 3 in the air before placing three flattened middle fingers on the closed lid of the piano. Apply pulling cycles at first, adjusting their size and shape to allow your fingertips to maintain contact with the flat surface, sliding no more than three inches: upper arms retract, supple fingers slide backward, hands scoop, and wrists rise; fingertips retrace their sliding path as arms cycle forward to complete the pattern and prepare the next stroke. Repeat this pulling circular motion of the entire playing apparatus 20 to 30 times until the separate elements of the cycle become thoroughly integrated and natural and you can render the cycle easily and loosely, sliding lightly on the piano lid.

Next, reverse the direction to perform a like number of repetitions in the pushing direction, pulsating forward with sliding, flattened fingers; flexible wrists, acting as a gear between your shoulders and fingertips, permit the back-and-forth sliding movement within a continuous, recurring, cyclical movement. Note that wrists move vertically with no lateral circling, and that the shoulder girdle actively initiates and sustains the action.

When the cycles feel comfortable in both directions, try them at the keyboard. Place the middle three fingers of both hands on the groups of three black keys nearest middle D, close to the fallboard. Apply pulling cycles at first, adjusting their shape and timing to create repeated, sustained, *mezzo forte* tone clusters. Five minutes of relaxed experimentation is usually sufficient to overcome an initial strangeness in accommodating these cycles to the realities of key length and depth on the instrument. Once you have succeeded in sounding tones by cycling in the pulling direction, learn to produce them in the pushing direction as well. Keep your shoulder girdle released to the outside at all times; this frees your upper arms, which remain close to the body when leading these cycles, to move easily in the shoulders. Make a conscious effort to maintain minimal tension throughout your entire body.

Upper arms supported by the shoulder girdle are the prime movers of a good piano technique. When the musical pace is sufficiently slow, as with the majestic chords of Chopin's C-Minor Prelude or in the heartfelt sounds of his E-Minor Prelude, upper arms gracefully initiate each key depression as part of a recurring, cyclical movement.

Experiment with these movements on the Chopin excerpts, playing all notes with cycling arms. Do pushing cycles in the first example (**Ex. 2-1**), and pulling cycles in the second (**Ex. 2-2**). Start each of the pulsating strokes with prepared, straightened fingers that, depending on the direction of the cycling, descend diagonally forward or backward into the keys. Each follow-through merges with the subsequent preparation as fingers slide back and forth. The continuously moving arms provide the power and control to create a wide range of opulent sonorities. By adjusting the size, shape, and pace of the cycles, you can generate, control, and sustain a slow-moving tempo that also engenders a sense of line, melodic shape, and forward motion.

Example 2-1. Play each chord with a continuously moving pushing arm cycle; fingers slide forward on the keys. Adjust the size, speed, and timing of the cycles to accommodate the sonority and pacing you wish to create.

Chopin, Prelude in C Minor, mm. 1–3.

Example 2-2. Play all notes with relaxed, slow (to make soft sounds), and continuous pulling arm cycles; fingers slide backward along the keys as you stroke.

Chopin, Prelude in E Minor, mm. 1–3.

8 A Pulling Arm Legato—Pronating and Supinating Circles

The pulling arm legato adds lateral wrist (and shoulder) circling to the single plane, up-and-down wrist movements I recommended you apply to the Chopin excerpts in the previous section. The lateral wrist and shoulder circling allow for a greater subtlety of movement of the playing apparatus, which in turn frees movement of the arms along the keyboard, smooths connections, and eventually enables you to support various finger patterns that can be organized within the cycles.

Learn first to execute pronating cycles on octave Ds with thumbs (**Fig. 2-1**). Let both thumbs relax against the inside edges of your hands in line with your second fingers (**Fig. 2-1A**); do not waste muscular energy keeping the thumbs separate from the hand. Lean back so that, with actively pronated and somewhat extended arms, the sides of your thumbs touch the Ds near their edges (**Fig. 2-1B**). Ready yourself to swing the entire arm with each prepared key descent.

Stroke slowly downward with pulling-pronating circles, playing softly with minimal tension: upper arms (elbows) move downward (back), outward, and around; wrists descend as you play, their bottoms reaching lowest at the bottom of the key. The sensation experienced is that of playing with the inside edge of the entire arm. Observe the sliding friction, the pronating roll, and the large wrist and small shoulder circles. You can produce long, repeated sounds maintaining contact with the keys at the top of the circle with hand scoop motion (**Fig. 2-1C**). Ingrain the recurring cyclical movement by repeating octave Ds in place, then walk the arms outward playing white-key thumb scales for an octave and back.

By circling with each key, arms produce sustained sounds punctuated only by the tiny last-second hand "hop." The action resembles that of hopping on one foot. The lingering contact, the continuous arm movement, and the linearly conceived playing—all enhance the feeling of legato. Practice the above octave D, contrary motion, thumb scale at MM 60, then extend the range experimenting with various dynamics and increased speeds up to MM 160. To play louder, swing more quickly as faster individual key depressions produce louder sounds. To increase speed, decrease circle size. Perform these pronating circle movements with other flattened finger pairs as well (2s, 3s, 4s, and 5s), lifting unused fingers just out of the way.

Play pulling-pronating cycles with paired, double notes using fingers 1 and 5: place collapsed thumbs (as before) on octave Ds with tightly set palm 5s a white sixth (perhaps a fifth) away. Maximally flex your fifth-finger knuckles with small muscles alone, causing their mid-joints and nail joints to bend backwards; knuckle lines slope downward towards the thumbs. Repeat the keys in place to accustom yourself to the feel of the circular movement before moving outward, making sounds so close they seem pedaled. Extend the range, experimenting with dynamics and tempo.

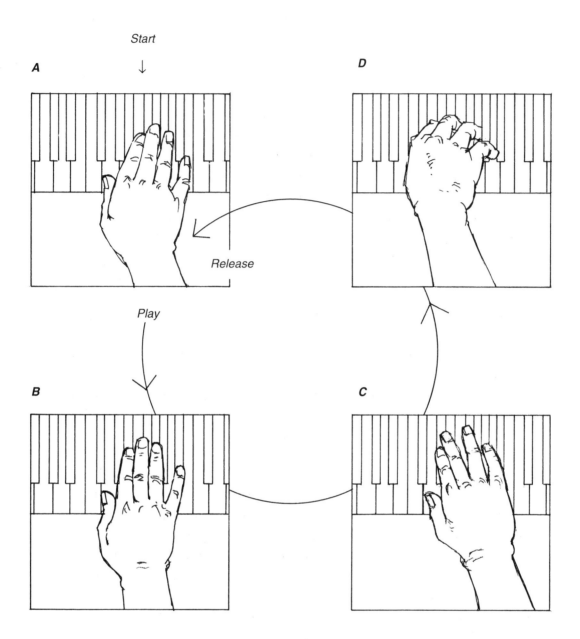

Figure 2-1. Pulling arm legato—four positions within a pulling-pronating circle (counter-clockwise motion for the R H shown).

A contrasting option **(Fig. 2-2)** calls for executing the pulling arm legato with 5s in the opposite direction, that is, with supinating cycles; arms remain loose and pliable throughout. Place the outsides of nonpronated hands on three-octave Ds (your hands are six octaves apart), allowing relaxed fingers to touch one another karate-style **(Fig. 2-2A)**. Again, waste no muscular energy holding the fifth fingers apart from the other fingers; the karate position automatically provides sufficient skeletal resistance to sound the tones. Lean back so that, with extended arms, fifth fingers reach the edge of the keys **(Fig. 2-2B)**. Stroke arms slowly downward with pulling-supinating circles using the outside edges of your hands—upper arms (elbows) go back, inward, and around; wrists descend sideways (hand adduction) as you play, circle inward, and around; ulna nobs, on the outsides of the wrists, reach their lowest point at the bottom of the swing depressing the key **(Fig. 2-2C)**. Pulsate the continuing circular movement, sounding sustained three-octave Ds in place at MM 60; then walk your arms inward playing white-key fifth-finger scales for an octave and return. Increase the range, experimenting with tempo, dynamics, and other finger pairs as well.

Try supinating circles on keys closer to middle D and pronating circles at the extremes of the keyboard. Both directions are more or less possible anywhere along the keyboard, but circling in the pronating direction occurs most often because of the natural affinity between pronation and extension. Supinating circles sometimes feel better when using the outsides of the hands and at the extremes of the piano. The musical context, the register of the piano, and chord voicing considerations all influence the decision to use pronating or supinating circles. Experiment with the various possibilities, realizing that the arms, with loose wrists and shoulders, are capable of sounding tones cycling in any pulling direction. You gain a wonderful sense of freedom, strength, and continuity by letting your upper arms and shoulder girdle take the initiative for individual key depressions. Try pronating and supinating circles on **Examples 2-3** to **2-7**, choosing the direction that feels best. Find other slow-paced melodies and choralelike examples to practice as well.

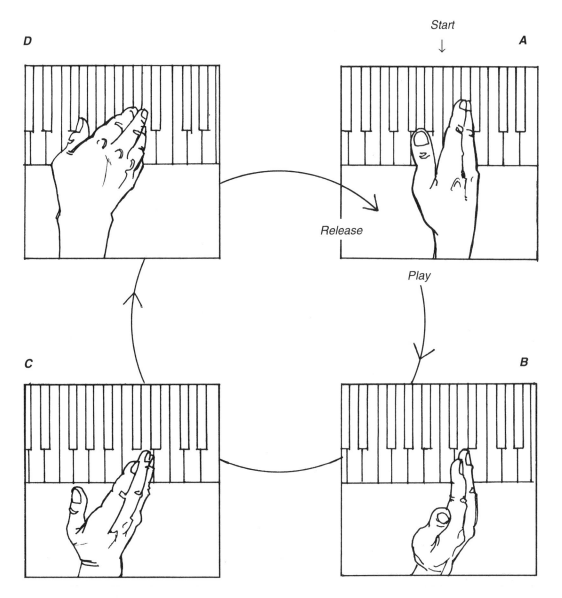

Figure 2-2. Pulling arm legato—four positions within a pulling-supinating circle (clockwise motion for the R H shown).

Example 2-3. Use gentle pulling-pronating arm cycles with continuous movement.

Schumann, Chorale, mm. 1–4.

Example 2-4. Use pulling-pronating cycles. Generate the necessary fullness of sound by pulsating each cycle very quickly at the point of key depression.

Mussorgsky, *Pictures at an Exhibition*, "The Great Gate of Kiev," mm. 61–65.

Example 2-5. Vary the speed of the key-depressing pulsations to fashion the tonal variety needed for shaping the longer phrase.

Beethoven, 32 Variations in C Minor, Var. 30, mm. 1–8.

Example 2-6. Use pulling cycles with each left-hand quarter note to mold the melodic line. Experiment with both pronating and supinating cycle directions.

Chopin, Prelude in D♭ Major, mm. 28–31.

Example 2-7. Gentle pulling-pronating cycles allow you to control the muted sonority.

Piston, Passacaglia, mm. 1–4.

8 B **Pushing Arm Strokes—Short and Long Sounds**

Pushing arm strokes are generated by the upper arms moving forward in the shoulders; hands move away from the body creating forward friction with the descending keys. You can produce energetic, moderately paced staccatos with great accuracy applying pushing arm cycles with straightened, prepared fingers. Review the sections on pronation extension (PM 2) and pushing arm cycles (IM 3) in Part One before continuing.

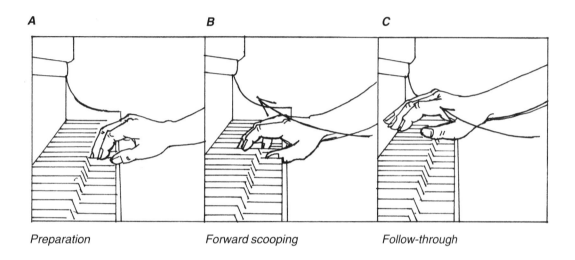

A   B   C

Preparation   *Forward scooping*   *Follow-through*

Figure 2-3. Pushing arm staccato.

Place thumbs and half-extended 5s touching white sixths, knuckle lines level, thumbs on octave Ds **(Fig. 2-3A)**. Stroke upper arms and shoulder girdle sharply forward, sliding and pronating along the keys **(Fig. 2-3B)**. This large, spoon-shaped gesture, representing half a cycle, both plays and releases the keys **(Fig. 2-3C)**; elbows move forward and outward. Relax instantly with the silence, letting gravity assist your hand's rapid return to the next key preparation; this represents the second half of the arm cycle. The motion resembles one that you would use to spin a free-wheeling bicycle tire away from you. Practice these prepared staccato thrusts in place at MM 60 to accustom yourself to the movement; then, when ready, move laterally along the white keys in contrary motion. Increase the range, experimenting with dynamics and tempo. This coordination, initiated by the upper arms and shoulder girdle, presents great advantages for control, power, and accuracy; learning to cycle your arms as rapidly as possible enlarges the opportunities for its intelligent use. Beyond a certain speed of repetition, of course, you must switch to a faster forearm movement. Apply these vigorous strokes to the following examples.

Example 2-8. Play each staccato eighth-note chord with prepared upper arm push strokes; fingers slide forward on the keys with elbows moving slightly outward. Keys are released as a follow-through of the forward playing motion.

Beethoven, Sonata in G Major, Op. 14, No. 2, second movement, mm. 1–3.

Example 2-9. The left-hand theme, connected by the damper pedal, gets its strength from the use of energetic, pushing upper-arm staccato thrusts.

Debussy, "Gardens in the Rain," mm. 43–45.

Example 2-10. Both hands use quick forward-sliding thrusts within a long pedal to build the massive resonance that is required.

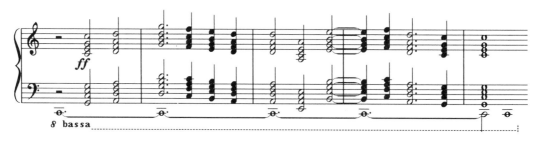

Debussy, "Sunken Cathedral," mm. 26–30.

Example 2-11. Pedaled left-hand pushing thrusts effect the resounding fullness and energy. Fingers slide forward on the keys.

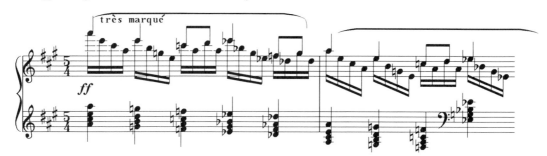

Ravel, Sonatine, third movement, mm. 54–55.

Example 2-12. Forward staccato thrusts in both hands within a long pedal produce this thunder.

Beethoven, Sonata in F Minor, Op. 57, mm. 17–18.

Use the pushing arm coordination to play moderately moving, unconnected single notes and complex chords securely at all dynamic levels. In particular, ingrain the kinesthetic feeling of projecting your hands, upper arms, and shoulder girdle so far forward, reaching almost to the fallboard. Many students find it strange, even difficult, to advance their upper arms to such an extent, mostly because their shoulders are too tight and they have been trained to stroke in a downward or pulling direction, never frontwards. Yet this ability to project upper arms appreciably forward prepares the next stage: while stroking, ride your wrists upward to lengthen contact with the keybeds. You now find that you can control sounds of any desired length. Experiment with various dynamics and note lengths. The following examples are germane.

Example 2-13. All notes except the sixteenths are played with separate pushing arm strokes, with prepared fingers sliding forward on the keys. Release forward, differentiating the lengths of the eighth and quarter notes.

Schubert, "Wanderer" Fantasy, mm. 1–4.

Example 2-14. Pushing staccato thrusts create the energy and humor. Generate the longer notes by raising the wrists during the stroke.

Schumann, "Whims," mm. 1–7.

Example 2-15. Energy, sonority, and accuracy of notes and rhythm are all improved by using a pushing arm thrust for each chord.

Brahms, Rhapsody in E♭ Major, Op. 119, No. 4, mm. 1–7.

To recapitulate: The pushing arm staccato, which always starts from the surface of the keys with straightened fingers, uses large, forward, spirited upper-arm and shoulder-girdle cycles to produce sharp (long with pedal), accurate, moderately paced sounds. Slowing the gesture and combining it with an upward wrist movement, which controls and lengthens finger contact at the keybed, converts the coordination to the standard, pushing arm stroke, a most direct and propitious approach to the instrument. The exaggerated forward thrusting practice has conditioned the player's shoulders, shoulder girdle, and upper arms to accept the simple arm-push stroke as completely natural.

These forward thrusts rarely involve supinating cycles; they either move directly forward or are accompanied with pronation. Cycling in the pushing direction, with arms moving outward from the body to depress the keys, minimizes keybedding; it encourages swift releases and quick preparation shifts. Pulling arm cycles, on the other hand, generate releases that are more complex and slower and, if the player is not careful, releases that can lead to keybedding, tightening in the shoulders, and tension in the neck and upper torso.

8 C **Upper-Arm Gravity Drops**

In the upper-arm gravity drop, a portion of the pulling arm cycle is combined with as much free fall as practical to generate full, maestoso sonorities. There are two forms of the coordination: a low-wrist form and a high-wrist form. Both require that the upper arms be freely released in the shoulders and that they be close to the body. Review the pulling arm cycles of IM 3, which you first practiced on an imaginary wheel, before proceeding to the low wrist option, the purer of the two forms.

Place 1s and 5s on the surfaces of white sixths, knuckles level, thumbs on octave Ds. Unwind your upper arms by pushing the imaginary wheel handles several inches away from you, and pause: upper arms move forward, forearms barely flex, and hands pull back **(Fig. 2-4A)**. Suddenly, cut all shoulder support to your arms, letting them fall instantly: flattened fingers slap the keys with low wrists and pulling friction **(Fig. 2-4B)**. Fight the tendency to reach out with hands or fingers, setting these elastically only at impact to transfer momentum to the key beds. Wrists—low before, during, and at the bottom of the fall—recoil instantly as shoulders retrieve the arm weight **(Fig. 2-4C)**. The higher the preparation, the louder the sound. Memorize the sequence—preparation, free fall, elastic recoil. Practice the coordination in place until the action feels thoroughly established, then walk laterally on white keys in contrary motion, experimenting with dynamics and tempo.

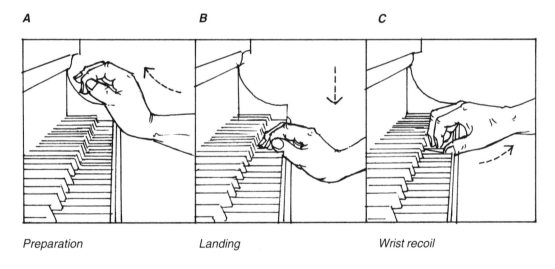

A   B   C

Preparation   *Landing*   *Wrist recoil*

Figure 2-4. Upper-arm gravity drop—low wrists option.

The high wrist form of the coordination involves less free fall and more muscular contraction of the large back muscles to speed the pulling upper arms. Place 1s and 5s as before on white key sixths: unwind your arms, but not your hands and fingers; wrists rise to their limit as fingers remain touching the key surfaces as close to palm position as the disposition of the notes allows (**Fig. 2-5A**). In this poised position, unwind your upper arms (push forward) an additional small amount before suddenly executing the vigorous dropping and pulling stroke at the shoulders (**Fig. 2-5B**). Fingers hold (extend and grab) near palm position; wrists, lowering only slightly during the stroke, recoil instantly to their original high position, this time forward, as shoulders retrieve the arm weight (**Fig. 2-5C**). The exertions, supported by strong muscles in your back, are extrememly powerful and necessarily short-lived. This coordination is potentially capable of producing the grandest chordal sonorities in the pianist's arsenal, but learn the movements playing softly to *mezzo forte* at first. Pace your efforts to delay fatigue or tension; the shoulder girdle remains released to the outside throughout with the shoulders completely free and upper arms hanging close to the body. Imprint both forms of the upper-arm gravity drop. When you feel ready, try **Examples 2-16** to **2-19**.

A　　　　　　　　　　　B　　　　　　　　　　　C

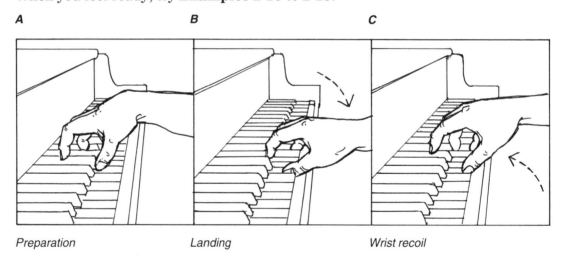

Preparation　　　　　　　　Landing　　　　　　　　Wrist recoil

Figure 2-5. Upper-arm gravity drop—high wrists option.

Example 2-16. Use relaxed, low-wrist upper arm gravity drops on each quarter beat to generate a deep, sonorous texture. Incorporate as much gravity in the drops as possible.

Brahms, Rhapsody in G Minor, Op. 79, mm. 1–3.

Example 2-17. Use low-wrist pulling gravity drops to project the left hand octaves that occur on the first beats.

Schumann, *Carnaval*, "Valse noble," mm. 1–6.

Example 2-18. Use the pulling high-wrist upper arm gravity drop here on every written note to fashion the thunderous reverberations. Keep elbows hanging near your body, and land fingers as close to palm position as the stretches allow. Wrists give slightly with each stroke and instantly recoil, but remain high throughout.

Mussorgsky, *Pictures at an Exhibition,* "Bydlo," mm. 38–44.

Example 2-19. Use high-wrist upper-arm gravity drops on every note to render this passage with power and precision.

Chopin, Scherzo in B♭ Minor, mm. 5–9.

8 D **Multi-Note Arm Patterns—Finger Stretching**

Heretofore each whole arm cycle, no matter the direction, has generated a single note or chord. I now introduce some additional applications of cycling arms in which a single arm and shoulder-girdle cycle propels or causes two or more successive key depressions.

Use supinating circles to play two-note outside/inside legato patterns in pull/push cycles. Begin by playing two-octave Ds with pulling karate 5s; circle inward, stretching thumbs as you go, to play octave Ds as part of the pushing phase of the arm cycle. Continue to circle around the broken octave, sounding two notes to each full arm cycle. Stop and reverse direction to perform pronating circles; ingrain both patterns. Experiment, cycling in both directions, with using intervals of different sizes. Ultimately the musical context will determine the paths of your arms. Try the examples below, using supinating cycles, and find other examples as well.

Example 2-20. Play each of the gentle two-note slurs (in both hands) with supinating circles. The first note is played pulling, the second pushing.

Brahms, Waltz, Op. 39, No. 9, mm. 1–6.

Example 2-21. All notes in each of the first two measures are played within a single pulling-supinating circle. The third measure calls for circling three times as fast—with each quarter note. The continuous arm movement, even at varying speeds, helps to energize and propel the music.

Schubert, Impromptu, Op. 90, No. 2, mm. 115–120.

Example 2-22. The left hand is played with slow, pulling-supinating half-note cycles.

Chopin, Nocturne in F Minor, mm. 1–4.

Now try the following multi-note examples that call for cycling in the pronating direction. Look for other practice examples.

Example 2-23. The right hand circles gently in the pronating direction with each broken chord to control the sound and pace the tempo.

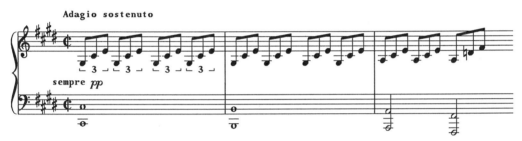

Beethoven, Sonata in C♯ Minor, "Moonlight," Op. 27, No. 2, mm. 1–3.

Example 2-24. The right hand repeated Bs are played in groups of two with pulling-pronating circles; thus the single off-beat Bs are played pushing with an extended fifth finger. The rocking motion helps to pace the movement.

Chopin, Prelude in B Minor, mm. 1–4.

Supinating circles with parallel, supporting forearm action are also used to assist the speed and accuracy of large outside-to-center shifts, which occur, for instance, in the traditional waltz or oom-pah bass. Practice a large outside-to-inside elbow snap motion one hand at a time; circle inward from a pulling karate 5 on three-octave D to a pushing palm thumb on octave, then middle D. Play and shift in one quick motion of the entire arm, continuing around to prepare the next arm snap. Remember the lesson of PM 6, which recommended that forearms supinate simultaneously to increase the speed of the inside lateral motion. Repeat this motion a dozen times with each hand separately to gain accuracy and to imprint the kinesthetic feeling of moving the entire arm so rapidly. Try the following examples that call for quick, supinating left-hand shifts.

Example 2-25. Use fast, supinating circles to play each measure of the left hand. The low note is played with a dipping, scooping motion that throws the hand to the inside; well-timed forearm supination speeds this movement.

Chopin, Waltz in E Minor, mm. 33–37.

Example 2-26. Use supinating quarter-note cycles to play the left hand. The bottom notes are pulled and scooped inward from a karate position, the upper chords are played pushing.

Brahms, Capriccio in B Minor, Op. 76, No. 2, mm. 1–4.

Example 2-27. Supinating circles with parallel forearm action help negotiate this difficult left-hand passage.

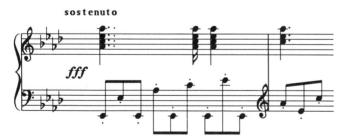

Chopin, Nocturne in C♯ Minor (middle section), mm. 49–50.

Practice the gesture in the opposite direction; large center-to-outside shifts require the use of pronating circles of the upper arms and forearms to reinforce and speed the movement. Practice two- and three-octave jumps with each hand in both directions until they become thoroughly ingrained and reasonably accurate. You must take special precautions (perhaps spreading your feet) to stabilize your body while doing these large, quick arm shifts. Apply the movement to the following examples and others you can find.

Example 2-28. Play each left-hand melody note with pulling-pronating circles to create the necessary power and intensity.

Schumann, Symphonic Etudes, No. 6, mm. 1–2.

Example 2-29. Use quick pronating circles to play the right-hand extending fifth finger line. Note the supinating circles called for in the left hand.

Rachmaninoff, Rhapsody on a Theme of Paganini, Var. XXIV, mm. 1–2.

Example 2-30. Here is a similar rapid pronating pattern, except in this instance the melody is played by the right-hand thumb.

Liszt, "La Campanella," mm. 4–7.

Pianists often negotiate large lateral spaces between the fingers, a situation that can occur in chords or with notes sounding singly in broken chord patterns. The supinated position of the hands and arms eliminates much of the strain normally inflicted by laterally stretching fingers because it allows flexing, rather than abducting, movements of the fingers to cover lateral keyboard distance. Experience this idea in the following instance. Place 5s on two-octave Ds with knuckles level **(Fig. 2-6A)**; in this position stretching 4s even a third away is strenuous. However, with supinated hands 4s can flex to easily span a fourth or fifth **(Fig. 2-6B)**. Play these 4s pushing, and circle the two notes. Stop, reversing to pronating circles. Do not confuse a supinated hand and arm position with the arm's ability to circle in both supinating and pronating directions!

A   B

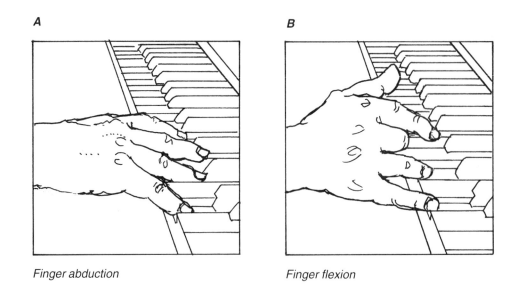

Finger abduction   *Finger flexion*

Figure 2-6. Supinated finger stretches.

So when you find yourself confronted with widespread legato intervals, extend your fingers and supinate your hands and arms; then circle upper arms in the direction that feels most comfortable, while keeping your hands supinated to ease the strain on reaching fingers. Try the examples below.

Example 2-31. After setting the supinated position of the hand to ease the finger stretches, play pronating circles in both hands. Thus the quarter-note melody and bass lines are played pushing forward.

Chopin, "Harp Etude," Op. 25, No. 1, mm. 1–2.

Example 2-32. Supinate the left hand to cope with the stretches, then pick the cycling direction that works best for you.

Beethoven, Sonata Op. 10, No. 3, first movement, mm. 23–26.

Example 2-33. Pick the circling direction that works best for you.

Debussy, "Movement," mm. 11–13.

Example 2-34. Prepare the left hand finger stretches with a supinated hand position, then circle in the pronating direction.

Chopin, Nocturne in C♯ Minor, mm. 1–3.

Example 2-35. Experiment to see which left-hand direction feels best.

Dohnanyi, Postludium, mm. 1–3.

Example 2-36. Here is a left-hand situation calling for both a supinated position and supinating circles.

Beethoven, Concerto in G Major, first movement, mm. 266–267.

Example 2-37. Here is a famous left-hand example calling for a supinated hand position moving in pronating arm circles.

Chopin, Sonata in B Minor, fourth movement, mm. 207–209.

Section 9 Forearms

In this movement category, forearms, moving in their elbow hinges, stroke the keys; upper arms and shoulder girdle provide sufficient support to create forward friction at the key surface. Firm your hands and straightened fingers just enough so they form a unit with the forearms. Straight-line, diagonal, front-to-back motion results as wrists remain still and upper arms move in a single vertical plane. Strokes, often begun from above, incorporate as much free fall as possible.

   Remember to take time before each exercise to set a good postural alignment with shoulders releasing to the outside.

9 A Forearm Bounce on Palm Finger—Correspondence

In this fundamental exercise, forearms bounce on supported palm-positioned fingers that are optimally arranged with respect to the hands and arms. I use the term *correspondence* to denote this alignment. When a finger is in correspondence at a particular place on the keyboard, the finger, hand, and arm are so arranged as to give the finger its maximum strength. Before moving on, review the trombone slide and washboard movements of PM 5 (the forearm push stroke) to recall the diagonal approach of the arms **(Fig. 2-7)**.

A   B

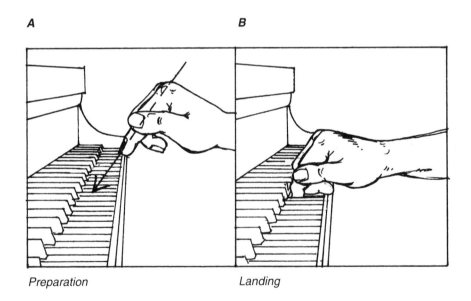

Preparation   *Landing*

Figure 2-7. Forward diagonal path of the forearm stroke.

Begin the exercise by placing second fingers in supported palm position. To do this, pronate fists, then unfold second finger nail and midbones, but not knuckle bones, until they are roughly perpendicular to the hands; 3s, 4s, and 5s remain loosely folded under. Press thumbs against the sides of the second fingers for added stability. Then place the tips of 2s on depressed octave Ds to set the correspondence (**Fig. 2-8A**).

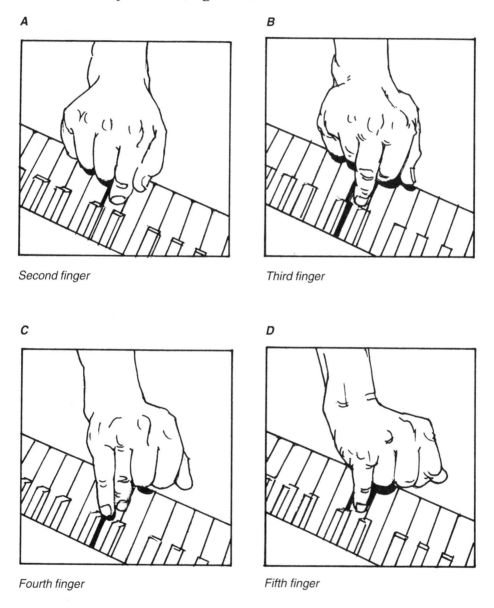

A

Second finger

B

Third finger

C

Fourth finger

D

Fifth finger

Figure 2-8. Fingers in palm and correspondence position.

1. Adjust wrists slightly to the inside to center your forearms behind the second fingers (hands abduct).
2. Adjust wrists vertically to align your straightened finger phalanges with the diagonal direction of the stroke.
3. Pronate arms sufficiently to position fingers minimally inside the vertical: elbows move away from your body adding an outward dimension to the forward diagonal stroke.

Palm second fingers are now in correspondence, optimally positioned to support your bouncing forearms.

Play paired forearm strokes on octave Ds in the gray area of the keyboard at MM 100; bounce an inch off the keys with no flopping of the wrists. There is a thrown, ballistic quality to the motion. Ingrain the diagonal stroke in place, playing *mezzo forte*, then walk double pairs (four repetitions) of bouncing notes outward on white keys to two-octave Ds and back. Insure that your two sides look and feel alike, that the bounce is energetic, that the sounds are rhythmically and dynamically even (watch especially the note before a switch), and that the lateral arm movement is smooth and well-coordinated. Do additional work on the weaker arm, carefully pacing youself to rest at the onset of even a slight fatigue.

Practice other finger pairs in turn, setting them first in palm, then in correspondence position. Arrange 3s as you did 2s, unfolding their outer bones from a loose fist while other fingers remain folded under in the fist; squeeze thumbs against 2s for added support (**Fig. 2-8B**). Compared with the second finger, wrists are positioned somewhat less to the inside and lower in this setting, and the arms are more pronated. Perform the same double pairs of bouncing repetitions moving laterally outward and back on white keys with your third fingers.

When setting 4s, the shorter 5s should also unfold and stiffen outward, adding to the thumbs' stabilization support of the landing finger (**Fig. 2-8C**). Correspondence requires that your wrists move decidedly outwards and lower with considerably more arm pronation. Perform the same exercise with 4s as you did with 2s and 3s.

Set 5s similarly to 4s, taking care their hand knuckles remain tightly flexed (**Fig. 2-8D**); all other fingers retain their loose-fist position. Wrists are extremely low and to the outside with hands completely adducted to the inside and arms drastically pronated. Accustom yourself to this awkward but significant position by bouncing more times on both 4s and 5s; notice the added outside angle of the stroke. Squeeze thumbs towards 5s for support; as the tips of 5s are back under the hand, be sure to extend your upper arms to reach the gray area. Do extra practice on the weaker and less coordinated side.

Next, bounce thumbs in palm and correspondence position on the same white key pattern. Locate this position by setting your fingers in the rounded pattern of PM 7, then curling the other fingers under and out of the way. The thumbs' aligned palm bones remain tightly flexed throughout the exercise; wrists are high and to the inside with minimal pronation.

Having bounced on all your supported palm-finger pairs, repeat the exercise and gradually eliminate the lateral thumb support. Train your landing fingers to hold with their own tightly flexed hand knuckles. Begin by bouncing lightly, insuring that the first phalanxes of the palm-positioned fingers do not drift away from the palms. Add sonority only gradually. Switch from one finger to another, then switch from one register to another, anticipating and imprinting the various correspondence positions. Over a period of time increase the lateral bouncing range to three-octave Ds, and add blacks. Give extra attention to the weaker arm or fingers. Speed the lateral motion by doing single pairs of bounces on each key, then single notes, executing the faster lateral movement as smoothly as possible. Rest at the onset of any fatigue.

Practice the following examples using forearm drops on palm-positioned fingers in correspondence.

Example 2-38. Play each of these notes with a forearm drop on palm finger, adjusting the correspondences as you go.

Bartok, Suite, Op. 14, second movement, mm. 1–8.

Example 2-39. These clangorous sounds are best rendered by using forearm drops on palm-positioned fingers in faultless correspondence.

Copland, Fantasy, mm. 10–13.

Finally, do forearm bounces playing palm 1s and 5s together on white key sixths with wrists high and middle fingers tucked under (**Fig. 2-9**). I call this the *resting position*. Make the necessary figure-eight adjustments (PM 6) to keep all fingers playing in the gray area: knuckle lines stay level and parallel to the fallboard. Experiment with dynamics and tempo.

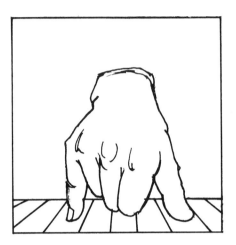

Figure 2-9. Resting position.

9 B **Lateral Forearm Skip**

To execute large, lateral shifts using the forearm bounce motion, the upper arms must perform two simultaneous tasks: they lead the sideways motion, and they support the vertical playing. To provide a sufficient foundation for this, your body must be firmly grounded in central position as the large reaching and destabilizing movements made by the shoulder girdle and upper arms require an exceptionally firm base.

Do the exercise indicated in **Figure 2-10** beginning on octave D with your right-hand second finger set in palm and correspondence position. Carefully center yourself in good postural alignment, spreading your feet apart on the floor for additional stabilization. Play two strokes per note at MM 80 on the entire pattern, proceeding stepwise downward, as indicated, for several notes. When the movement feels completely comfortable, eliminate the repetitions to double the lateral speed. Upper arms lead the lateral motion in both directions in a pattern similar to the figure-eight movement in PM 6. Avoid being overcautious; it is better to miss a note occasionally than to interrupt the flow of your arms. Inch the metronome up to MM 100, working for speed and accuracy. At faster speeds, imagine that your thrown hands are pulling the arms. Perform the mirror image of the entire exercise with your left hand.

Figure 2-10. Forearm lateral exercise pattern.

Practice the lateral jumping exercise with your other right-hand fingers, including your thumbs, in palm and correspondence position. It takes courage to jump palm 5 on black keys, but the effort is instructive! Do the mirror image of the entire exercise with your left hand, spending extra time on the weaker arm and on unsure fingers. Take another opportunity to equalize your finger, arm, and shoulder-girdle development.

Finally, perform the pattern, still one hand at a time, with palm 1 and 5 on white-key sixths in resting position **(see Fig. 2-9)** and with 5 on the written note. Sticking to white keys, play double then single strokes on each key. Jumping 1 and 5 requires constant wrist shifting and arm turning to keep both fingers landing in the gray area. Remain centered at the piano and repeat these changes until the figure-eight modifications become thoroughly instinctive and automatic.

9 C **Foward Gravity Drops—Rebounds**

Place 1s and 5s in resting position on white-key sixths, thumbs on octave Ds. Bounce your forearms a dozen times before stopping to lightly hold the keys. The bouncing encourages ballistic movement whose instant release guards against keybedding, or late, unnecessary pressure on the bottom of the key. Next, pivot your arms forward and backward over the lightly held fingertips to find a suitable point of equilibrium. You will find this point to be with wrists held high. Check that your shoulder girdle is released to the outside and that your upper arms fall close to your body before continuing.

Retract forearms slowly with hands and finger hanging; the upper arms withdraw as well; pause with your fingers some four inches above the keyboard (**Fig. 2-11A**). Suddenly, throw (let go of) your hands and forearms forward retracing their upward path (**Fig. 2-11B**); fingers grab for a split second at impact and hold lightly again. Did you get the sound you expected, or wanted? Repeat the drops in place until they feel ingrained. Vary the dynamics by altering the speed and height of the drops, and walk white-key scales out laterally in contrary motion. Extend thumbs to sevenths and octaves without changing the free-fall aspect of the coordination. When necessary, point middle fingers out front to help reach the wider intervals, but always keep your wrists high when performing forearm drops.

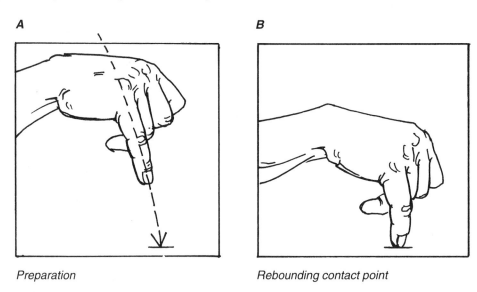

A

B

Preparation

Rebounding contact point

Figure 2-11. Forearm gravity drop—rebounding position.

Rebounds are loose, close, controlled repetitions that follow a forearm gravity drop as aftertremors; elbows alone move while wrists, hands, and fingers are firmed just enough to move as a unit with the forearms. Rebounds generate a natural diminuendo as the single, unrenewed larger impulse runs out of steam. Insure that the last note of a rebounding group is neither late (lazy) nor accented (as though a new impulse were starting).

Do single, double, and triple rebounds which, when added to the initial drop, produce units of two, three, and four sounds. Practice forearm drops at MM 48 as indicated in the pattern in **Figure 2-12A** using fingers 1 and 5 in resting position on white-key sixths. Time the drop so that the landing (grasping) of the fingers at the bottom of the keys coincides with the click of the metronome; fingers remain there until a subsequent click signals an arm retraction. Play the pattern in **Figure 2-12B** at the same tempo as **Figure 2-12A**; after an exaggerated drop, execute the second note softly, hinging your elbows without letting fingers leave the keys. Move on to **Figure 2-12C and 2-12D**, performing them in similar fashion. Maintain the slow tempo, treating each measure as a cluster unit to be ingrained.

Figure 2-12. Rhythmic exercise routine for rebounding.

Increase speed gradually to MM 100 and practice anticipating an exact number of sounds. Experience the power and ease inherent in this ability to throw a controlled number of vibrations with one large, gravity-aided impulse. It is especially important here that your shoulder girdle be relaxed outward in order to free your arms for the gravity drop and rebounds.

Extend the interval to an octave and insure that the wider stretches do not interfere with the freedom of repetition. This coordination has many uses including dotted-note playing. Try these examples and find others in your music to practice as well.

Example 2-40. The repeated eighth notes should be played as slow forearm rebounds to keep the rhythm precise.

Schubert, Sonata in G Major, Op. 78, third movement, mm. 1–6.

Example 2-41. The hands alternate single forearm rebounds, making tonal richness and precision relatively easy.

Mendelssohn, Variations serieuses, Op. 54, Var. XII, mm. 1–3.

Example 2-42. The sixteenth notes each begin a forearm rebound unit of two repetitions to generate striking declamatory strength.

Barber, Sonata, mm. 1–2.

Example 2-43. All right-hand octave eighth notes are rendered as forearm rebound groups of five repetitions, creating both authority and excitement.

Schumann, *Carnaval,* "Valse allemande," mm. 9–12.

Example 2-44. The left-hand motive groupings that occur at this climactic point can be powerfully rendered by using the forearm rebounding coordination.

Beethoven, Sonata in F minor, Op. 57, first movement, mm. 130–131.

Example 2-45. Forearm rebounds generate power and rhythmic energy here.

Brahms, Ballade, Op. 10, No. 2, mm. 1–5.

Section 10 **Hands**

This movement category concerns hand flexion (and extension), the vertical hand movement responsible for key descent. Wrists are double-hinged joints that allow for both vertical and lateral movement. When the two movements are performed simultaneously, the wrists can do some circling. You will find that the hand-bouncing motion presented in this section is identical to the scoop movement of PM 8 but whereas the hand scoop motion of PM 8 began with low wrists and fingers touching the keys, the bouncing motion described here starts above the keys with high wrists that become even higher as the fingers land with backward friction on the keys.

10 A **Hand Bounce**

Bouncing hands produce faster and lighter repetitions than bouncing forearms. These scooping hand vibrations are possible only when fingers are firmed with small muscles alone (a position usually indicating that fingers are straightened close to the palm position). If you firm your fingers with the long muscles located in the forearms, the tendons that pass through the wrist become taut and prevent your hands from bouncing freely in the wrist. Hand bounces work most efficiently with high wrists.

Rest palm thumbs with high wrists lightly on the keybeds of octave Ds, other fingers remaining folded under (**Fig. 2-13A**). Retract hands slowly, moving in the wrists alone, until the tips of the thumbs are several inches above the keys (**Fig. 2-13B**). Pause, checking that shoulders, elbows, and fingers are still, but not rigid. Loosely throw your hands forward and under, incorporating as much free fall as practical; fingertips inscribe an arc and create backward friction with the keys (**Fig. 2-13C**). Rest and return; repeat the motion until it feels completely natural.

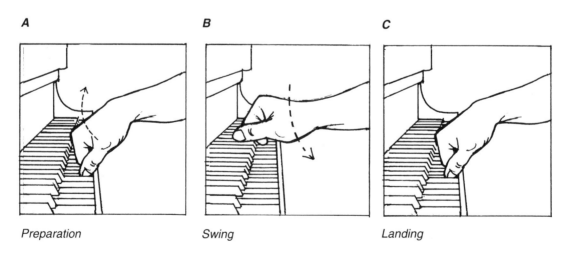

A   B   C

Preparation   *Swing*   *Landing*

Figure 2-13. Hand bounce.

Establish the measured bouncing rhythm as indicated in
Figure 2-14 on octave Ds, MM 100 to a quarter note, then work your way
outward on white keys for an octave and back. Gradually increase speed to
MM 160 playing softer and bouncing the hands closer to the keys. Here is
another example of how reduced motion increases the potential for speed.
Your hands hinge loosely in the wrists while your thumbs stay firm, moving
as part of the hand.

Figure 2-14.   Rhythmic exercise pattern for hand bounce.

Do the sequence with each of your other finger pairs set in palm
and correspondence positions. As long as palm fingers are held by the small
finger muscles located below the wrists in the hand, wrists are free to bounce.
When ready, move from key to key without interrupting the eighth-note flow;
do four, two, then single bounces on each note; extend the range and vary the
dynamics. Add black keys to the routine and insure that the two hands look
and feel alike. Play hand bounces on white-key sixths with 1s and 5s in resting
position, making the needed figure-eight modifications. Give the weaker fingers
or arm extra practice, pacing yourself to never push beyond a slight level of
fatigue. Always rest before resuming practice.

Hand bounces may be combined with single forearm gravity drops
to create a series of controlled repetitions. Do forearm drops first with palm 1s
and 5s on white-key sixths rebounding in the elbow; gradually relax your wrists,
allowing your hands to bounce. Alternate the two coordinations to imprint the
contrasting kinesthetic feelings. Hand rebounds are lighter, faster, and looser
than forearm gravity-drop rebounds, and they create backward friction with the
keys. Throw forearms and hands together to start a group of hand repetitions.
Begin with a group of three, and gradually increase the number of hand
rebounds off one arm impulse to seven or more; as you vibrate, ride wrists up
and upper arms forward. See **Example 2-46** for a natural application of this
idea. Experiment with this coordination using other finger combinations and
intervals up to an octave.

Hand bounces may be combined with upper-arm pull/push cycles
to produce continuous, pulsating repetitions. Place fingers 1 and 5 in resting
position on white-key sixths, thumbs on octave Ds. Play single sounds at first,
alternating arm directions and rocking your wrists back and forth. When the
push/pull pattern feels ingrained, begin to bounce twice in each direction
renewing energy on the pull side. Accustom yourself to the combination in place
before walking laterally in contrary motion. Working calmly, slowly, and with
little sonority, do three, then four bounces to each half of an arm cycle. When
ready, increase the speed, but not the dynamic level. Spread the interval to an

octave; again remember to keep your hands as limp as possible, to play lightly, and to never practice these movements beyond a slight level of fatigue; rest before resuming practice. Your endurance will increase gradually over time, and should not be forced. Try the hand-bounce motion on the following examples, and on other similar passages.

Example 2-46. The five fast right-hand octave repetitions are rendered with a combination of the hand bouncing, the arm riding forward, and the wrist vibrating upward.

Mussorgsky, *Pictures at an Exhibition,* "Two Polish Jews," mm. 15–16.

Example 2-47. The eighth notes in both hands are rendered with hands bouncing in the wrists for grace and control.

Schubert, Sonata in A Major, Op. 120, first movement, mm. 117–118.

Example 2-48. Both hands lightly bounce the sixteenth notes to fashion the gentle murmuring.

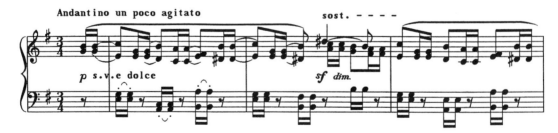

Brahms, Intermezzo, Op. 119, No. 3, mm. 1–3.

Example 2-49. All sixteenth-note groupings, those involving both three and five repetitions, are accomplished with hands loosely bouncing at the wrists while the upper arms move forward. This lends potency and precision to the passage.

Rachmaninoff, Prelude in G Minor, Op. 23, No. 5, mm. 17–18.

Example 2-50. The excitement is created by hands bouncing in the wrists on each staccato sixteenth note, whether the notes repeat or change.

Mussorgsky, *Pictures at an Exhibition,* "The Market Place," mm 1–2.

Example 2-51. All sixteenth notes in both hands are produced with hand bounces. The repeated right-hand thumbs must be integrated with the eighth-note motion of the top line; stamina is an important issue here.

Schumann, *Carnaval,* "Reconnaissance," mm. 1–4.

10 B **Scoop Chords**

Scoop chords are prepared, staccato chords played with extending forearms, pulling upper arms, and scooping hands stroking simultaneously. These combined actions speed key descent, creating the potential for producing sounds of great force and sharpness. Practice this type of chord stroke on the simple triad inversions in **Figure 2-15**, playing mezzo forte and staccato. Prepare the triads two octaves apart in the following arrangement: touch your shorter fingers in the gray area, your longer (middle) ones in the black; set outside fingers in palm position with knuckles sloping down to claw thumbs. With hands formed in this manner, stroke each pair of chords several times. Play the chords with arms moving parallel, and chromatically to the right and back, between the indicated chords.

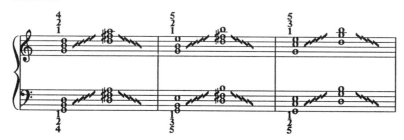

Figure 2-15. Exercise pattern for scoop chords.

Stroke keys sharply, using a simultaneous arm-press and hand scoop; you can improve the leverage by starting with lowered wrists. Scoop your hands far and sharply enough to kick your arms and hands off the keyboard, a movement resembling the hand scoops of PM 8. Note the possibility for using this coordination on the following examples.

Example 2-52. All chords can be played accurately and in full control of both loudness and length, by using hand scoops.

Schumann, Symphonic Etudes, Var. 3, mm. 1–3.

Example 2-53. The wide dynamic ranges possible with hand scoops can be put to good use here on the repeated chords.

Beethoven, Sonata in D Minor, Op. 31, No. 2, first movement, mm. 163–168.

Return to the triad exercise **(Fig. 2-15)** and play the individual chords with fingers sounding separately in contrary motion, but maintaining parallel chordal motion. Drop with low wrists on outside fingers in palm position; sound the remaining two notes by scooping hands under with little perceptible finger action: upper arms and forearms, of course, resist the forward tug; wrists ride up, thumbs play on their heads, and fingers finish under the hand. Complete the exercise playing contrary broken chords continuing in this same way.

Next, drop on claw thumbs with low wrists to scoop in the opposite direction, to outside palm fingers. Play the entire exercise pattern performing each broken chord in like manner. Experiment with various dynamics and speeds. Notice how gently pulling arms and hand-scoop pressure are able to create, largely on their own, a pulling finger legato: the combined movements propel your carefully positioned fingers (this is important) almost without their knowing it. There is certainly little feeling of independent finger stroking or releasing. This type of flexible, weight-transfer motion, initiated by scooping hands, provides a promising basis for playing more-complex legato passages. Find musical excerpts, such as the ones below, where you can apply this principle.

Example 2-54. These may be treated as scooped broken chords.

Beethoven, Sonata in E♭ Major, Op. 27, No. 1, second movement, mm. 1–10.

Example 2-55. The muffled drum beats in the left hand are accomplished with the hand scooping carefully preplaced fingers.

Gottschalk, "Union," mm. 149–150.

Section 11 **Thumbs**

In this movement category, independently stroking thumbs effect key depression. Connected to the hands near the underside of the wrists and well behind the other fingers, the thumbs' unseen, double-hinged, palm knuckle joints are capable of both vertical and horizontal movement, and in combination, circular. The vertical movement necessary for ordinary key depression requires that the thumbs forego their instinctive grasping response to swing sideways. This adduction, when compared with the customary flexing of other fingers, feels weak and a little strange. In other circumstances, however, a natural flexion does propel their horizontal movement, which greatly facilitates lateral shifts along the keyboard and the spanning of chords.

The primary disadvantage of the thumbs is their shortness. Nevertheless, various correspondence manipulations can compensate for this disadvantage, including arm pronation, lowered arches, abducted hands, and playing longer fingers near the fallboard. When the thumbs are employed landing on their heads in resting position, they can and do play in the stronger flexing direction, a uniqueness the pianist should certainly exploit. Students often need special instruction in swinging thumbs from their primary connection to the hand, especially in the vertical plane. Some of them may also need help with a collapsing midjoint problem, a serious condition causing both weakness and inflexibility of the thumb.

11 A **Thumb Movement—Adduction and Flexion**

Drop forearms on white-key fourths or fifths with 1s and 5s in resting position, thumbs on octave Ds, their bones in line **(Fig. 2-16)**. With arms propped on 5s, raise your thumb tips vertically about 1 inch above the keyboard, moving only in the palm-knuckle joints; pause, then stroke forward and downward: tips curve and scoop. Begin an even adductive movement at MM 50, increasing speed in stages to MM 132. Stroke as high as the tempo allows and play notes to either side as well. Repeat the exercise placing thumbs in claw position with low wrists; the movement range is considerably reduced, but you experience the same sideways feeling that accompanies all vertical thumb movement.

On their heads, thumbs can and do play by flexing across the key. Perform a forearm drop on white-key sixths with 1s and 5s in resting position, thumbs on octave Ds **(Fig. 2-17A and B)**. While holding lightly, flex (squeeze) fingers 1 and 5 toward each other, then retract forearms three inches **(Fig. 2-17B and C)**. Practice this exercise in four counts: drop on ONE; flex fingers 1 and 5 on TWO; retract forearms on THREE; remain poised on FOUR. Gradually compress counts ONE, TWO, and THREE, until the sixths become staccato.

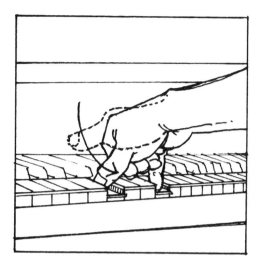

Figure 2-16. Vertical thumb stroke.

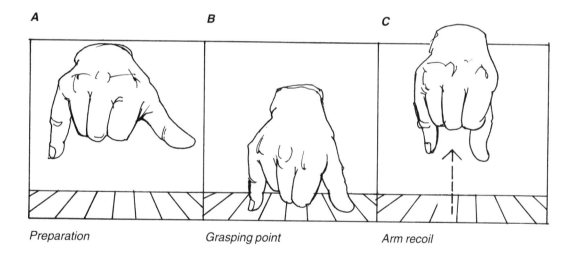

A   B   C

Preparation   Grasping point   Arm recoil

Figure 2-17. Grasping thumb stroke.

Become accustomed to the new pattern: bounce on the count of ONE, remain poised on TWO. Once the forearm-finger timing is worked out, the *grasping touch* feels particularly natural and strong because both fingers flex together with their palm-positioned bones in line. It is an exceedingly efficient coordination, especially with its possibility for instant release. Grasp various intervals up to an octave working thumbs against other fingers; practice to perfect the timing between grasping fingers and dropping forearms. Seek places in your music to apply this highly effective touch.

11 B **Collapsing Midjoint—Lateral Thumb Movement**

Occasionally students must overcome the physical problem of having a thumb midjoint collapse inward without control; this condition seriously hampers the lateral freedom of the thumb and allows much of the thrust intended for the keybed to be dissipated (**Fig. 2-18A**). The solution to this problem is to gain conscious control of the palm bone extensor, the muscle located in the forearm that pulls the palm phalanx with its midjoint out and back from under the middle of the palm; the palm becomes flatter, the arch lowered. In moving towards claw position, the thumb's midjoint cannot collapse. Perform the following exercises to gain this control.

A B

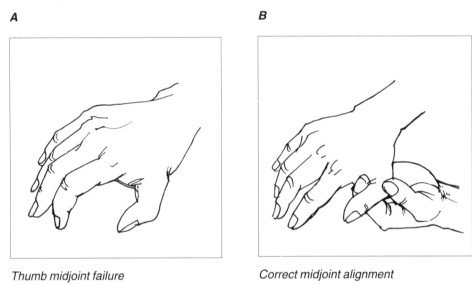

Thumb midjoint failure   *Correct midjoint alignment*

Figure 2-18. Collapsed thumb midjoint.

1. Grasp the midjoint on the thumb of the right hand with the first two fingers of the left hand and stretch the palm bone back to its limit (**Fig. 2-18B**). Let go of the midjoint and force the palm bone's own extensors to hold the midjoint in place. Repeat the exercise several times, increasing the time span, but do not let fatigue accumulate. Reverse hands to work with the left thumb midjoint.
2. Place both hands in extended position. While holding your palm bones firmly back, flex the mid- and nail joints of both thumbs to claw position; alternate the two positions.
3. While holding a tight claw position, work palm knuckles in the vertical plane.

These exercises gradually strengthen the palm bone extensors, giving a student conscious control over the midjoints. In time the problem of collapsing midjoints should be eliminated.

Thumbs have a special role in scale playing. It is important therefore to carefully integrate their movements with those of the arms and fingers. First, do a slow preparatory trill: place claw thumbs with low wrists on the surfaces of octave Ds; stroke sharply with arm-push support and rising wrists. Sound second fingers gently by lowering wrists; release thumbs and imprint this thumb-second finger cycle. Next, play contrary white-key legato scales for an octave and its return, using the same two fingers; thumbs are passed-under and prepared. Pronate arms and abduct hands when stroking thumbs; supinate and adduct hands when playing 2s. Ingrain these combined movements, then do identical contrary scales with fingers 1 and 3. Repeat the exercise with fingers 1 and 4. This combination of actions may be used as a model for slow-to-moderate speed scale playing with, of course, the supination spread over the two or three nonthumb notes of the scale.

Play claw 1s and 5s on white-key fifths with palm bone extensors contracted and arches low; stroke thumbs vertically to experience their relative strength, but minimal swinging range. Walk individual thumb strokes out to an octave, playing soft, close staccatos: to do this, you must open thumb midjoints, abduct your hands, and pronate your arms. Rest at the onset of any fatigue. Return beyond the original interval of a fifth, making opposite adjustments and note how vertical movement becomes increasingly difficult as thumbs move near, then under the palms. The implication for rapid scales and arpeggio playing is clear: rather than reaching under second fingers with thumbs, shift (lift) the entire arm quickly to the outside to place thumbs on their keys in the new position beside (not under) second fingers.

11 C **Flexibility and Correspondence**

Thumbs continually adjust to changing arch levels and hand slopes, and to the pronation that accompanies the stroking arm. Review the hand and arm calisthenic exercises IM 2.1-2.3, to recall how supple and relaxed the thumbs must be to efficiently integrate with your rotating arms. The basic finger action involves shifting from palm 1 and 2 to claw 1 and 2 and back **(Fig. 2-19A and B)**. Practice this alternation in the air before going any further.

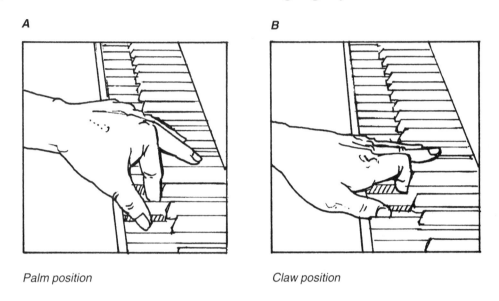

A

B

Palm position   *Claw position*

Figure 2-19. Thumb flexibility.

Drop on white-key thirds with palm 1s and 2s, thumbs on octave Ds. Collapse these two fingers diagonally forward to claw position, integrating the exchange of position with diagonally moving (trombone slide) forearms: as you descend forward into the keyboard, palm bones withdraw, second fingers collapse, arches and forearms lower, and fingertips slide apart. Repeat the back-and-forth motion until it becomes loose and pliable, and until the combination of arm and finger movements feels fully integrated and natural. Similar adjustments are necessary to mesh thumbs with rotary arm action: pronating arms tilt fingers 1 and 2 towards claw position; supinating arms towards palm position. Thumbs must dovetail with these surrounding movements over and above those actions they take to sound their own keys.

Do a final lateral exercise **(Fig. 2-20)**: the purpose here is to increase the range and ease of lateral movement of the midjoints and palm-knuckle joints of the thumbs and to integrate this comfortably with the movement of the upper arms. Students often exhibit the debilitating but curable problem of tight thumbs with limited lateral range that force them to negotiate legato crossover movements by awkwardly thrusting their upper arms and elbows outward.

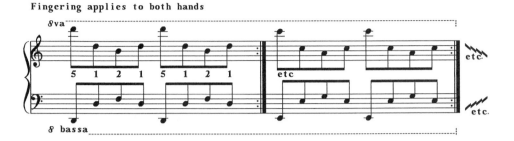

Figure 2-20. Lateral thumb flexibility exercise pattern.

Play the exercise using low wrists which circle legato in the supinating direction: hands pronate as 5s play the outside notes **(Fig. 2-21A)** and supinate as they move to the inside **(Fig. 2-21B)**; thumbs play and shift simultaneously as mid- and palm-knuckle joints overflex to create sufficient lateral range. Exaggerate this flexing movement of the thumbs to avoid forcing your elbows clumsily outward, a malcoordination that is cured simply and instantly by unlocking the thumbs. Walk the flapping pattern inward and back on white keys, leaning back when arms pass in front; work for increased speed and agility. Flexing your thumbs sufficiently allows your elbows and upper arms to shadow the lateral flow of the notes in extended passages. As the notes go outward, your elbows go outward; when the notes go inward, the elbows likewise follow. Free and extensive lateral movement of your thumbs encourages a natural lateral flow of the arms, and in so doing, contributes enormously to the melodic fluency of your playing.

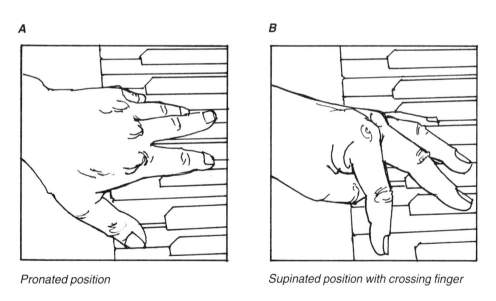

Pronated position   *Supinated position with crossing finger*

Figure 2-21. Lateral thumb movement with arm rotation.

Section 12 **Fingers 2 Through 5**

Up to this point fingers have been employed largely as part of the hands or forearms, or positioned to act as passive extensions of the whole arm; one exception is the grasping motion against thumbs, which was presented in Section 11 A. In the movement category now under consideration, fingers swing independently in their hand knuckles to depress the keys. Before proceeding, review the theory of finger movement as presented in PM 7 and elaborated in PMs 8, 9, and 10. Rework the hand and arm calisthenic drills, PM 7.1–7.5 and IM 2.1–2.3.

Moving predominantly at the knuckle, fingers consist of three phalanges and two additional joints; each can be controlled separately. The knuckle is a modified ball-and-socket joint whose principal action—flexion—moves vertically; limited lateral movement is possible only in extended position. The mid- and nail joints are simple hinge joints and though capable of flexing with the knuckles, they need not be; their considerable independence allows for subtly differing finger strokes and shapes.

12 A **Pulling Finger Strokes**

Efficiency and strength in finger movement, as elsewhere, depend largely on correspondence relationships with the arms. These relationships vary for each finger and for the same finger in different registers. The core positions for each finger were first presented in Section 9 A, "Forearm Bounce on Palm Finger." Review these essential elements of correspondence, for the same alignment principles of the finger, hand, and arm apply as well to the swinging finger coordinations of this section. Then proceed to the first of the four pulling finger strokes that are discussed—flexing fingers activated by small muscles alone.

1. *Small muscle squeezing stroke* (**Fig. 2-22**). Begin with second fingers: place flattened second fingers on the surfaces of octave Ds at the fallboard (**Fig. 2-22A**). Create long sounds by drawing or sliding 2s under towards you; the small muscles in the hand, working alone on the first or knuckle phalanx of the fingers, pull them to palm position between the black keys which serve as fences. Mid- and nail joints remain totally passive and bend backward; forearms rise along with the knuckle arch (**Fig. 2-22B**).

    Ingrain this squeezing-type stroke. The ability to flex your knuckle phalanges, which are controlled by the small muscles in the hand, without flexing your mid- and nail phalanges, which are controlled by the long muscles in the arm, is of considerable import: it signifies your conscious ability at any time to will loose wrists and fingers and your effective control of the ever-changing proportions of small and long muscle application.

    The black key fences aid the search for correspondence: over-adducted hands cause fingers to bump outside fences; over-abducted hands cause fingers to bump inside fences. Overpronated or oversupinated arms create similar problems. These alignments interact and are functionally acceptable when fingers are able to flex parallel to their keys. Discover, practice, and memorize these important positional arrangements for all your finger pairs. Remember, positions change not only for individual fingers in a common register but, because of the lateral, figure-eight hand and arm adjustments, they differ also for the same fingers in various registers. Learn to do this squeezing stroke on assorted Ds with your other finger pairs as well.

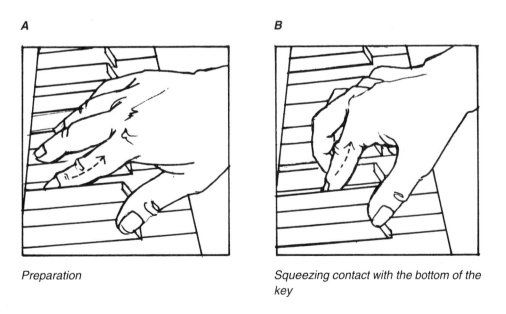

A   *B*

Preparation   *Squeezing contact with the bottom of the key*

Figure 2-22. Pulling fingers—the small muscle squeezing stroke.

2. *Finger snap stroke* (**Fig. 2-23**). Using the correspondences reaffirmed in the small muscle squeezing stroke, play staccato finger snaps with second fingers. Release the keys by continuing the pulling-scooping playing gesture of the fingers. Maintain finger shape not by stiffening the finger, but by timing your long and small muscle pull: begin by scooping your fingertips (**Fig. 2-23A**), then continue the stroke by flexing largely in the hand knuckle (**Fig. 2-23B**). Ingrain light snaps at first, then execute more vigorous, but spaced finger strokes. Louder sounds require more proportional exertion of the long muscles. Take care to set your shoulders no more than necessary, and relax between efforts to avoid any build-up of tension or fatigue. Practice other finger pairs with correct correspondences on Ds in various registers. When snapping 5s, it is decidedly advantageous to keep 4s tucked under the hand; become aware of and accustom yourself to this phenomenon.

A **B**

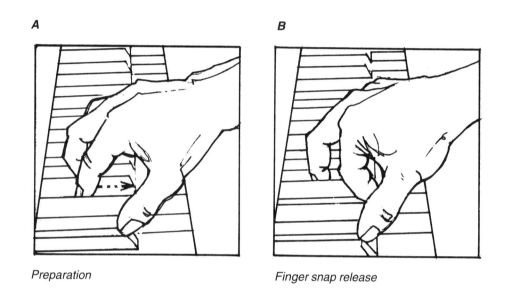

Preparation   *Finger snap release*

Figure 2-23. Pulling fingers—the finger snap stroke.

3. *Scratch touch stroke* (**Fig. 2-24**). Place second fingers in exaggerated palm position lightly on the bottoms of octave Ds. Vibrate the tips back and forth, making quick repeated sounds; fingers neither leave the keys nor allow them to surface completely. The tiny scratching motion has little if any up/down feeling. Set correspondences carefully, for even minor miscalculations affect efficiency. Practice other fingers pairs on Ds in this and other registers.

   The first three pulling finger stroke exercises all begin with prepared fingers touching their keys. Their practice promotes positioning, control, flexibility, speed, strength, and subtlety in your finger movements.

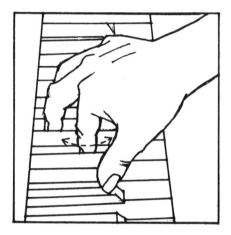

Figure 2-24. Pulling fingers—the scratch touch stroke.

4. *Unprepared pulling finger stroke* (**Fig. 2-25**). Perform the unprepared finger strokes with thumbs lightly holding the edges of octave Ds in claw position; place second fingers a minor third away, then cover adjacent white keys with successive finger pairs. To begin, adjust to second finger correspondence with elevated arches, and insure that your palm-bone midjoints are out and back (**Fig. 2-25A**). Swing second fingers briskly from one inch above the keys, stopping abruptly to hold lightly at the bottom (**Fig. 2-25B**). Note the curvilinear stroke, the scooping friction, and the upward kick at the knuckle. Note also that the other fingers are able to swing freely with and behind the active second fingers. Wrists and elbows function as stationary fulcrums, but be sure to maintain this hand and arm stillness with minimal tension. Practice the exercise in three counts: swing on ONE; hold lightly on TWO; raise fingers loosely, but sharply, one inch on THREE.

   Do other finger pairs while thumbs rest on the bottoms of their keys. Take care with 4s and 5s to adduct hands, lower wrists, and pronate arms sufficiently—all while gently holding thumbs. Practice these coordinations and positions in all registers until they feel natural and become automatic. Change to a simple ONE-TWO, down/up pattern when cured of any keybedding tendency. Scoop nail joints at the point of contact and hold keys lightly. Remember that the loudness of the sound is controlled by finger and key depression speed, not by the amount of tension or pressure on the bottom of the key. Decrease the stroking arc to speed repetitions. Switch back and forth to various finger pairs while lightly holding thumbs to imprint the changing correspondences; note these positions well, for they underlie the execution of an efficient, effective legato.

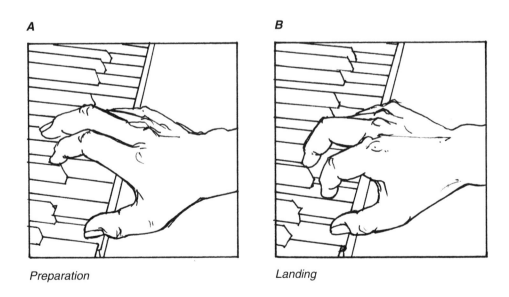

A

Preparation

B

Landing

Figure 2-25. The unprepared pulling finger stroke.

12 B Collapsing Fifth Fingers—Lateral Strength

Some students find themselves coping with fifth finger knuckles that sag so badly as to make it impossible for the finger to swing independently. Held needlessly high and curved with ill-positioned arms and hands, these helpless digits play as extensions of lunging arms **(Fig. 2-26A)**. To swing independently in the key playing direction, 5s require the exaggerated correspondence described earlier in Section 9 A: low wrists, fully adducted hands, highly pronated arms, inflated arches with their fingertips touching well behind 4s **(Fig. 2-26B)**. Accustom yourself to this exaggerated position. In general, you must learn to favor the shorter fifth fingers, not by substituting arm for finger strokes, but by positioning hands and arms, however fleetingly, to encourage their productive, independent movement.

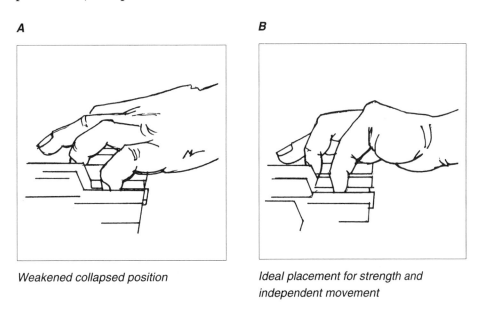

A

B

Weakened collapsed position

Ideal placement for strength and independent movement

Figure 2-26. Collapsed fifth-finger knuckle.

To cure collapsing fifth fingers, hold your hands in extended and pronated position in front of you; swing extended 5s up and down in the air, letting the other fingers follow. If the knuckle needs freeing, reinflate either hand's arch by pressing the second finger of the other hand into the palm just behind the crease line of the problem knuckle (**Fig. 2-27A** and **B**). Move to the keyboard and continue this support. After setting the proper correspondence, play octave Ds in the white area with various pulling touches. Many students find this first experience at independent fifth-finger movement a revelation. After a few days of such practice you should be able to eliminate the artificial support. As long as the correspondence for the finger stroke is correctly set, the arch should remain inflated on its own.

A　　　　　　　　　　　　　　　　　　　　**B**

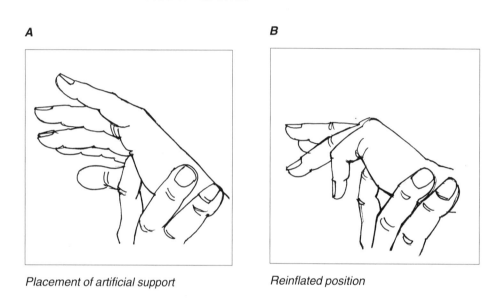

Placement of artificial support　　　　　　*Reinflated position*

Figure 2-27. Reinflating fifth-finger arch.

Fifth fingers, as the outside edges of the hands, need considerable lateral strength, particularly when the hand is in supinated position. Play two-octave Ds in karate position, the fingers' full length touching along the keys (**Fig. 2-28A**). Remain in the supinated position and abduct your hands: fifth fingers slide backward along the keys to produce a fanlike spreading of the fingers; stop when 5s are vertical (**Fig. 2-28B**). Reluctant arms apply a slight isometric counter pressure, but do not pull back or withdraw from the keyboard. Return to your starting position by adducting your hands. Pace the repetitions to avoid any build-up of tension or fatigue.

Begin the next exercise by performing the first half of the previous one; when 5s are vertical and hands fully abducted, simultaneously pronate your arms and flex your fifth fingers to palm, pivoting lightly on the finger tips **(Fig. 2-28C)**. Pronate until you land with claw thumbs playing white keys a sixth away with arches that slope downward towards the thumbs. Retrace your steps—supinate arms, extend 5s, then adduct your hands returning to karate position. Repeat the combination until these integrated actions feel natural.

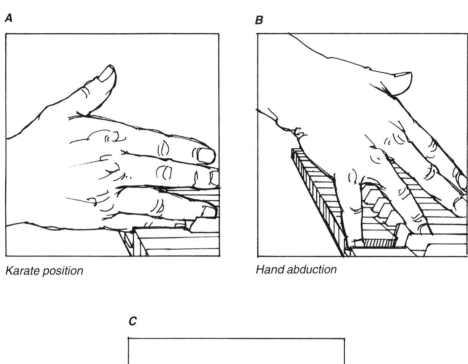

A

Karate position

B

Hand abduction

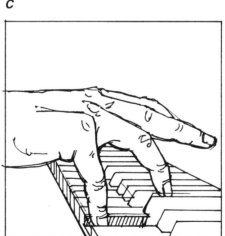

C

Pivoting towards a pronated position

Figure 2-28. Fifth-finger lateral strength.

12 C **Overlapping Legato**

Few skills contribute to the quality of piano sound more than a pianist's ability
to vary and manage the degree of connection between tones. This takes place on
a continuum having at one end an exceptionally short finger staccato and at the
other a well-regulated, overlapping legato, with various degrees of connection
between these extremes. The ability to perform a consciously controlled, overlapping finger legato enables pianists to enrich their sound in ways that are
more subtle than the use of the pedal alone.

Place claw thumbs lightly on the keybeds of octave Ds with your
other fingers touching the surfaces of adjacent, raised white keys. Perform
the overlapping legato exercise **(Fig. 2-29)** at MM 100: starting with thumbs
already down, swing unprepared 2s on the count of ONE; thumbs lift sharply
but minimally for one beat on the count of TWO, while the second fingers hold
lightly for three counts, and so on. Notice that each finger is playing dotted half-
notes interspersed with quarter rests and that the two fingers are a half note
apart. Strokes are vigorous and the releases, which occur during the other
finger's held tone, are sharp but not high. Hands and arms are quiet except for
the anticipatory correspondence shifts that are made with each release, and
which are designed to anticipate and prepare the ideal correspondence setting
for the next finger stroke.

Right hand shown.

Figure 2-29. Overlapping legato.

Practice other two-finger combinations at the slow pace and
accustom yourself to the correspondence placement of each finger. Next,
increase the tempo gradually; you will find that your fingers arc less and at a
certain stage separate correspondences become impractical. The result is a
correspondence setting for the trill or tremolo that lies between, or averages,
the model setting for each of the individual notes.

With more than two successive notes, arms proceed from one note-
pair average to the next. Their movement anticipates the new average setting,
thus preventing your fingers from reaching awkwardly or swinging disadvant-
ageously. This is a crucial point. The arms lead the movement, pulling the
fingers to the next position where they can comfortably make their own independent contribution. Legato thus implies continuous small movements of the
wrists and arms, whose shape is determined by the shape of the musical line
itself and its position on the keyboard. The general orientation is a microcosm
of the larger figure-eight arm adjustments of PM 6; movement to the outside

calls for hand adduction and arm pronation; movement to the inside calls for hand abduction and arm supination; arms cycle forward and back as well to help with finger placement. Therefore, a decision about fingering, which prescribes specific physical gestures of the hands and arms, becomes a decision related to musical realization. Ultimately, it leads not only to subtle control of phrasing and sonorous effects, but opens up a path to the very heart of the music.

Play the following four-note patterns in two tempos: (a) slowly enough to do a controlled overlapping legato; (b) then fast, creating a circular movement of the arms which allows them to support close fingers by traversing average correspondences of successive note-pairs.

1-2-3-2	1-2-4-3	1-2-5-4	2-3-4-3
2-3-5-4	5-2-4-1	5-2-3-1	3-4-5-4
5-3-1-3	3-2-4-1	4-3-1-2	4-3-4-1

You will find that your arms, if they are loosely hanging from shoulders that have been released to the outside, will instinctively produce the cycles needed to support the correspondence movement. Add to these recurring arm cycles a subtle and flexible hand scoop, weight-transfer pressure to help you shape the dynamic possibilities inherent in the linear movement.

Here are some practice examples that can profit by cyclical arm support of the fingers; find other examples in your music and elsewhere.

Example 2-56. The repeated sextolets are best performed with circular arm-support movement based on moving average finger correspondences.

Ravel, *Le Tombeau de Couperin*, Prelude, mm. 1–3.

Example 2-57. Arms cycle and pulsate to renew the energy.

Beethoven, Sonata in F Minor, Op. 57, third movement, mm. 15–19.

Example 2-58. The right hand quickly cycles behind each group of light triplet-sixteenth notes.

Debussy, "Movement," mm. 1–3

Example 2-59. Circling your right arm makes this soft, fast passage relatively easy.

MacDowell, "A Haunted House," Op. 61, No. 5, m. 28.

Example 2-60. Arms cycle to support the left-hand recurring finger patterns.

Beethoven, 32 Variations in C Minor, Var. 10, mm. 1–2.

Example 2-61. The right arm cycles to support and shape the recurring quarter-note sextolets.

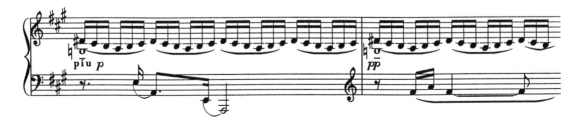

Debussy, "Joyous Island," mm. 20–21.

12 D Unfolding Finger

The *unfolding finger* is the second of the two basic directional strokes of the fingers. It proceeds from the claw position towards palm position as described in PMs 7 and 10.

Begin by placing claw-positioned hands on the bottoms of adjacent white keys, thumbs on octave Ds (**Fig. 2-30A**): fingers are exaggeratedly curved, palm bones back, arches low, wrists high as upper arms tilt forward. Withdraw arms along the trombone-slide diagonal by slowly unfolding fingers to palm position without releasing the keys; arches and forearms raise (**Fig. 2-30B**). Go back and forth between the two positions to imprint the alternating action and to integrate the arm and finger movements. This motion is identical to that described for fingers 1 and 2 in Section 11 C, "Flexibility and Correspondence," except here all fingers are included in the exercise.

Stop midway between claw and palm position and slowly allow the keys to surface. Begin to softly play repeated thumbs without their leaving the key surface. Then, holding thumbs lightly, practice other glued finger pairs with proper correspondence: fingertips push outward from the palms stroking with forward friction, but without sliding; mid- and nail joints unfold during the key descent and recurve with the key release. This is the standard unfolding finger coordination at the keyboard; strokes are prepared, finger movement is minimal, and arches are as high as the shorter fingers permit.

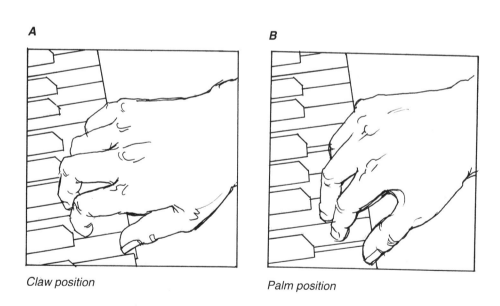

A   *B*

Claw position   *Palm position*

Figure 2-30. The unfolding finger stroke.

You can reproduce this coordination with flattened hand and spread fingers: touch the surfaces of convenient triple-blacks with flattened middle fingers near the fallboard, covering whole tones to either side with the outside fingers of your hands. Repeat single finger pairs that never leave the keys: stroke by unfolding fingers to create forward friction; blend in correspondence angles and ingrain the movements. Use this coordination for extended arpeggios, like those in the examples below:

Example 2-62. Flat, spread, unfolding right-hand fingers, backed by a smooth weight-transferring arm movement, help to make this passage work. Fingers touch the keys on their pads well behind the fingertips and even so, create forward friction with an unfolding finger action.

Debussy, "Reflections in the Water," m. 24.

Example 2-63. Flat, left-hand, unfolding fingers make this roaring accompaniment work. The techniques for negotiating the arm shifts will be discussed in Part Three.

Rachmaninoff, Prelude, Op. 23, No. 2, mm. 1–2.

The same unfolding finger action is used to preset fingers that become extensions of forward-stroking arms. By differentially setting individual fingers, you can voice a chord to varied specifications, accentuating, for instance, any note(s) of a triad—top, middle, or bottom. The fingers are set before the arms or hands reach the keys. Even when functioning as part of a larger unit, the fingers must anticipate and ultimately control the subtleties of tonal balance.

Rest claw-positioned fingers on the surfaces of adjacent keys. Suddenly, simultaneously press your arms forward and spring your fingers, catapulting your arms out of the keys. This action needs short, quick, forward arm support. It is especially valuable when quick takeoffs are needed for rapid shifts. Except for the direction of the force, unfolding (springing) fingers and pushing arms accomplish goals similar to those realized by hand scoops with snapping fingers and pulling arms. Unfolding fingers give you a forward option, one that meshes with pushing arms in the same way pulling fingers dovetail with pulling arms.

Do the overlapping legato exercise (Section 12 C)—originally intended for unprepared, pulling fingers—with prepared, unfolding fingers, and contrast the inner sensations and results. When the exercise is done with unfolding fingers, wrists are higher and looser (like rolling an orange), and keys feel heavier and under greater control (as small muscle use predominates). There is less tension, a closer legato, and the possibility for greater speed. What are missing, however, are power and brilliance.

Alternate pulling and pushing finger strokes with single pairs of fingers on octave Ds starting with 2s. Notice that both strokes aim towards palm position and that the direction of a particular finger stroke is predetermined by its previous release. Pulling strokes follow extending releases, unfolding strokes follow curving releases. Arms and fingers become reflexively entwined as fingers anticipate and react to the directional changes of arms, which in turn accommodate the changing finger needs. Operating largely subconsciously, these various movements fuse into a single, well-functioning, automatic system that remains on call, poised and ready to respond to your inner ear and musical imagination.

When pianists have attained a well-developed, flexible technique through intelligent practice, they will have in place a miraculously responsive playing apparatus: once they conceive the kinds of sounds and musical shapes they wish to produce, they will automatically produce them. If they imagine something subtly different, this too will be produced automatically and instantly without their having to worry about what muscles or coordinations must be altered. Such is the nature of a mature, adaptable technique that is grounded in musical values.

12 E Sidesaddle Walking—Substitution Practice

Two useful and important habits are reinforced by practicing a certain amount with hands turned inward 90 degrees, so that forward and backward movements of your arms carry your fingers laterally up and down the keyboard: (a) shorter fingers on the outsides of the hands are trained to play behind longer ones equalizing length and strength, and (b) arms move continuously to position unfolding fingers.

Turn your body 45° to the right, as if on a sidesaddle, and place left-hand palm 5 on middle D, with wrist low, hand adducted, and arm pronated (**Fig. 2-31**). Knuckle lines are perpendicular to the fallboard; let fingers 4 and 3 fall to their adjacent keys and proceed to play the exercise presented in **Figure 2-32**.

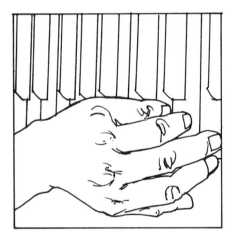

5 touches behind 4 which touches behind 3

Figure 2-31. Sidesaddle position of the left hand.

Figure 2-32. Sidesaddle exercise pattern.

Play lightly and loosely, with unfolding fingers, so that the keys feel heavy; float your arm on top of the fingers whenever there are three notes in one direction. Walk the pattern up white keys for an octave and return. Turn 45° left of center (left sidesaddle) to do the mirror image with your right hand. This exercise ingrains a strong disposition of the hand by forcing your outside shorter fingers to touch behind the longer ones. It also strengthens the outsides of the hands. Note that the shortest finger, 5, can always play straightened without concern for taking its neighbors out of range.

Resume right sidesaddle position: with your left hand beginning on octave D, walk a white-key legato scale alternating 2 and 3 up to three-octave D and back **(Fig. 2-33A and B)**. The arm glides forward to help fingers reach, play, and then collapse. Returning is more difficult as the withdrawing arm pulls flexible fingers behind one another. Fingers bend, unfold to play, and unfold further to reach the subsequent note; avoid lateral arm wiggling to help place the fingers. Practice extra on walking backward. When you have habituated yourself to a steady gliding motion, do the exercise with fingers 3 and 4, and hardest of all, with fingers 4 and 5. Perform the mirror equivalent with the right hand and devote more time to the weaker arm and to the less-coordinated fingers. Increase speed from MM 100 per note to MM 200.

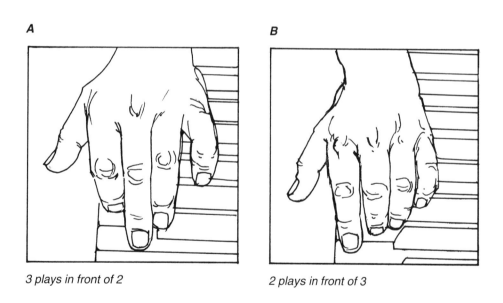

A

B

3 plays in front of 2   *2 plays in front of 3*

Figure 2-33. Sidesaddle two-finger walking.

In right sidesaddle position play the three-note pattern in **Figure 2-34** with your left hand, using two fingers only. Play lightly in pronated position with arms cycling above unfolding claw-shaped fingers. Keys feel heavy with arm and fingers fully integrated. Do the mirror image with your right hand while seated in left sidesaddle position.

Figure 2-34. Sidesaddle two-finger rocking.

For a final exercise, face forward again to do a type of finger walking I call substitution practice. This is an effective way to increase finger dexterity and nimbleness. The exercise calls for playing one-finger contrary white-key scales; the neighboring fingers substitute for the fingers that sound the notes, providing connection to the subsequent tones **(Fig. 2-35)**. Longer fingers touch in front of shorter ones. Hands angle to help; for fingers 1-2 and 2-3 they angle inward (adducting); for fingers 3-4 and 4-5 they angle outward (abducting).

Begin this exercise by touching 4s lightly on the bottoms of octave Ds. Play the outside neighboring notes with 5s **(Fig. 2-35A)**. Substitute these in front with 4s halfway to the next sound **(Fig. 2-35B)**. Continue outward in this manner to three-octave Ds; return by playing 4s and substituting 5s. Two nimble finger movements must take place for each new legato sound. Begin at MM 100 and increase to 200. Practice lightly to develop quickness; angling hands will help. Do the three remaining finger combinations. When completely comfortable with the motions, try some chromatic practice.

A

B

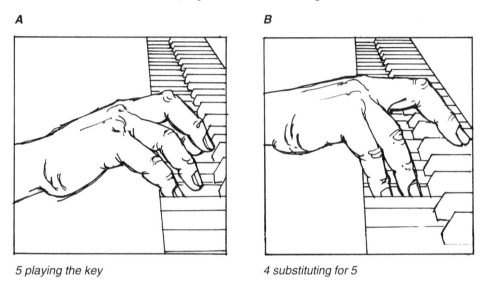

5 playing the key

4 substituting for 5

Figure 2-35. Substitution practice.

Section 13 **Summary**

The exercises and instructions of Part Two applied the biomechanics and learning concepts presented in Part One to the production of live sound at the piano. The progression from larger playing units, positions, and movements to smaller ones has been retained. The discussion of certain elements may be obvious to some students, or unwittingly taken for granted by others. I include such topics because they are part of the total picture; but they may not be part of everyone's knowledge. Your growing awareness of your own movements and movement abilities will help you decide for yourself just how much time you should devote to each section. My aim is to provide the information and training that allows you to construct a balanced and flexible technical base, one that permits and encourages you to develop organically in the course of normal literature practice. No two people will need exactly the same thing; it is for you to choose your own best path to this ideal.

Part Two established the upper arms with shoulder-girdle backing as the prime movers of a first-rate technique: they cycle along with flexible wrists in both pronating and supinating directions, play pushing and pulling, drop from above, and lead lateral movement. Supinating arm movement facilitates fast outside-to-inside jumps, whereas the supinated position of the hands eases the strain on laterally stretching fingers. Arms, articulating in loose, relaxed shoulders, take individual key depressions when possible; beyond this they cycle to systematically support the faster motion of smaller units. Be alert to any tightness and constraints in the shoulders, as this causes fatigue, stiffness, and a loss of power and accuracy. You can eliminate the problem by taking the time necessary, whenever you sit at the piano, to set a good postural alignment, especially in allowing the shoulder girdle to release (relax) completely to the outside.

Forearm and hand touches are differentiated by their elbow and wrist hinges and by their production of forward and backward friction on the keys. Choose the forearm touch whenever the repetitions are not too fast, because it is the stronger of the two coordinations and its approach angle allows for better control of tone lengths. With hands in resting position—high wrists with middle fingers tucked under—forearms lead gravity drops and rebounding activity. Hands can bounce with the synchronized support of the arms; they also lead in playing scoop-motion chords and in creating the subtle scoop pressure that supports a pulling finger legato.

Correspondence describes a positive, positional relationship between your fingers and your hands and arms, a relationship that varies with the finger, the shape and order of the notes, and the register. Flexible wrists and rotating arms make these alignments possible. Correctly arranging the various elements of your playing apparatus is the most direct road to increased strength, speed, and control, whether your fingers swing independently or are preset to become part of a larger playing unit. Fingers, like upper arms, are able to stroke in both pushing (unfolding) and pulling directions.

It is important that your outside fingers be able to swing independently as well as fulfill their role as strong but passive extensions of the arms. Broken thumb midjoints and sagging fifth-finger knuckles cause physical weaknesses and distortions that severely limit keyboard control and technical development. Sidesaddle walking and substitution practice develop strong positioning instincts of the hands and fingers. They integrate finger and arm movement, and promote finger strength and dexterity.

The coordinations of Part Two can now be increasingly applied to real music making. The intentionally simplistic note patterns I provided serve only to introduce a new coordination. The musical examples, expanding on this introduction, indicate where the coordinations might be applied in the traditional literature. Practice the movements on these musical excerpts, and as soon as possible find relevant passages in your own repertoire where they might also be applied. Where appropriate, the process can be reversed; that is, when confronted with a passage in your music that proves troublesome, analyze it technically, decide what elements are involved, and consult the appropriate areas and exercises in this book. The latter is a most valuable method of using the book.

Part Three   **Synthesized Movement**

Section 14 Introduction

If musical thinking and expression derive solely from our inner hearing, what has been gained by approaching technique from the vantage point of body mechanics? If technical proficiency embraces the idea of a smooth integration of the total playing mechanism, including the whole body, what has been gained by separating its component elements? These questions deserve answers.

Not all facets of piano technique, in the normal course of events, develop equally or in sequence; people differ and their growth patterns vary. Furthermore, the keyboard is itself unnatural, the movements it calls for relatively awkward, and the works of music normally encountered by piano students relate only indirectly to orderly technical growth. The standard "technical training" such as scales, chords, arpeggios, and studies, while doing much to teach keyboard familiarity, classical patterning, and basic theory, cannot guarantee well-integrated technical growth. The probability of healthy technical development in early-to-intermediate piano study is certainly lower than it should or could be.

By abstracting the elements of playing movement from their musical context, we encourage awareness of the relevant body mechanics. Thus for a limited but important percentage of the practice time, we focus attention on the purely physical processes of playing, giving it undivided, critical scrutiny. This aspect of piano study—the technical—will eventually be joined with other commensurately developed skills to achieve true musical and pianistic growth.

On the technical side it is possible to establish with reasonable dispatch a nourishing aggregate of movement habit, learning skills, and understanding that can be successfully applied to developing needs. If our movements are integrated, flowing, and within our control, then musically imaginative minds can direct their timing and goals. Without this inner harmony of coordinated movement, we will be musically frustrated.

Part One discussed fundamental movements, the building blocks of technique, in an objective, abstracted manner. It established a working vocabulary, increased self-awareness, and promoted the formation of simple, necessary movement habits to be acquired one step at a time. These components combined into larger coordinated patterns comprising the essential elements of piano-playing movement. Part Two linked these core patterns on an elementary level with sound production and musical idea.

Part Three, building on these concepts, presents a synthesis of the elements of good piano technique, elements that increasingly coalesce. Fingers join with arms and hands in integrated patterns emphasizing their fluid, harmonious mutuality. Subtleties of movement emerge that mirror the subtleties of the musical shapes encountered. Slowly, surely, and with normal, ordinary effort, a student will develop the flexibility, efficiency, expressiveness, and endurance to serve even the most demanding musical ends. Our vision in

140

performance cannot but be affected by our physical abilities: physical limitations restrict our musical imaginations just as increased physical skill spurs them. By training our bodies to do more—to create graceful, well-coordinated, even virtuoso movement—we expand the pianistic and artistic possibilities.

Section 15 **Legato Movements**

The section on legato movement focuses primarily on physically connected linear passages, and on the ways in which the arms facilitate the control, accuracy, sonority, and speed of the fingers managing these connected lines.

15 A **Joggle Movement—Chordal Repetition**

A movement that I call *joggling* implies a relaxed, subtle arm movement that underpins each and every connecting finger. When unnecessary tensions in the playing mechanism evaporate and the tempo is not too quick, pulling upper arms are able to unite with separately stroking fingers to produce strong, flexible, legato connections. This combined touch is particularly useful in executing slow to moderately paced notes that call for an extended dynamic range. By training your upper arms to move more quickly, in both the pulling and pushing directions, you enlarge the extent to which you can profitably apply this coordination. The purpose of the initial exercise is simply to integrate the pulling upper arm movements with individual connecting fingers.

Sit at the piano in a well-postured central position with shoulders released outward. Play the notes in **Figure 3-1** with prepared, connected fingers on white keys, 1 through 5 and back; use pulling-pronating arm circles for each separate finger at MM 80. The coordination, drawing on the arm movements described in "Pulling Arm Legato" (Section 8 A), uses slack, semicurved, relatively passive, pulling fingers reinforced by pulling and circling upper arms. Without maximal relaxation in your fingers, wrists, arms, and shoulders, your upper arms will be unable to pull backward with each sound. True connection, even controlled overlapping, is possible as lowered wrists transfer graded scoop pressure from finger to finger.

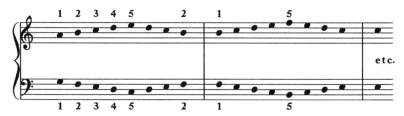

Figure 3-1. Joggle-action exercise pattern.

Practice **Figure 3-1** until the joggles feel completely natural and there is no difficulty resetting each finger-pair's proper correspondence in the slow tempo. Insure that you pronate sufficiently in moving to the outside to touch 5s on their inside tips before continuing on around back to your starting point; upper arms thus circle the larger note pattern in addition to joggling (small circling) on each note. Prepare increases of speed by joggling each pair of fingers several times in place (with arms cycling on a lightly held pivoting finger) before tying the movement to successive fingers; stay especially loose in the shoulders and fingers. Decrease movement size to gradually increase speed

142

until at about MM 200 your pulling upper arms reach a natural limit; faster movement must then be supported by a different coordination calling for greater forearm contribution.

Forearm joggles call for the arms' stroking angle to move forward. The hands become semiclawed (with higher wrists) as extremely supple knuckles dip and unfold with each joggle, allowing the fingertips to maintain a secure legato. Pushing forearm joggles require an even freer playing mechanism than the pulling upper arm joggles. Here is certainly an instance where excessive struggle can easily create tensions that interfere with the results; assume a casual-observer stance in working with these movements. Return the metronome to 80, and accustom yourself to the forward knuckle-dipping motion playing two forearm joggles to each click. Again, slowly increase the tempo: approaching MM 152, forearms begin to bounce; at faster tempos they vibrate.

Joggle action gives subtlety, ease, and strength to moderate connected movement by allowing the arms to back each fingered legato note. Without the benefit of this touch, a pianist must unhappily choose between playing softly on top of the keys, and suffering continual, tiring arm pressure. If the speed of the notes (and joggles) strains the pulling upper arms, change to forearm joggle action. Make these transitions as smooth and automatic as possible, striving to cover any discernible break in the rhythm or quality of the sound produced while switching from one form of arm motion to the other. Practice to gain mental control over the muscles you must release to make this coordination possible, to develop arm quickness in both directions, to integrate the movements with various kinds of finger patterns, and to control the significantly larger dynamic range now available to you for playing legato single-line quarters, eighths and sixteenths. A natural application of joggles is in playing legato double notes. Joggling allows you to apply, even in a fingered legato, the general rule that movement should be initiated, or at least buttressed, by the largest feasible unit, in this case the arms.

Practice joggling on various legato patterns in parallel scales and arpeggios, in appropriate places in your music, and in the examples below.

Example 3-1. Subtly and beautifully shape the right-hand line using a large upper arm circle for the wider phrase shape, and small individual note joggles for tonal variety and richness within.

Mozart, Sonata in A Major, K. 331, first movement, Var. 3, mm. 1–2.

Example 3-2. Forearm joggles help to express the shape of the lines and provide needed power, all while allowing the fingers to play a secure legato.

Chopin, Ballade in F Minor, Op. 54, (coda) mm. 211–212.

Example 3-3. Joggle forearms behind right-hand sixteenths for rhythmic and tonal control. The fingers, working independently along with the forearms, bounce out of the keys to produce the nonlegato.

Beethoven, 32 Variations in C Minor, Var. 14, mm. 5–7.

When notes move too fast for individual forward arm strokes, you may joggle every second note. This technique is particularly effective for expressing the running lyricism in Mozart's faster movements. See the following examples.

Example 3-4. Listeners must be unaware of the eighth-note joggles underpinning the sixteenth-note melodic movement; they should hear only the rich lyricism of the right-hand lines. Some passages in the sonata call for joggles every four sixteenth notes.

Mozart, Sonata in B♭ Major, K. 333, first movement, mm. 4–6.

Example 3-5. Joggle the right hand every two sixteenths; other places in the movement call for joggling every two or four sixteenth notes depending upon your inner hearing of the music.

Mozart, Sonata in A Minor, K. 310, first movement, mm. 23–25.

For even faster motion, you can joggle every third, fourth, or higher-aggregate note. These joggles approach the movements recommended for the multi-note arm patterns of Section 8 D, but here the arm movements do not necessarily match recurring ostinatolike musical patterns. Practice various gearing ratios, perhaps on scales, until your arms can instinctively support your fingers in assorted rhythmic units at all speeds.

Keep in mind that the joggle is not a jagged accent that cuts the line, but rather a loose, graded undulation that imparts energy, forward thrust, and sustaining power to the linear motion. Use this coordination to play ordinary legato quarters, eighths, and sixteenths (perhaps even thirty-second notes) in the traditional literature. If you find this idea novel, in applying it you will discover marked improvement in the efficiency, flexibility, and sonority of your playing. But remember, the joggle has no chance of working without your shoulders being released to the outside and your arms and fingers devoid of all unnecessary tension. This coordination must just "happen" as a release from effort; trying too hard is counterproductive. Play these examples.

Example 3-6. Joggle the right hand every three sixteenth notes.

Mozart, Sonata in C Major, K. 330, third movement, mm. 17–19.

Example 3-7. Joggle both hands every four notes, then every eight notes.

Beethoven, Sonata in C Major, Op. 53, first movement, mm. 25–27.

Example 3-8. Joggle the right hand every six notes, then every twelve notes. The left hand calls for using two pushing-pronating cycles per measure.

Chopin, Etude in F Minor, mm. 1–3.

The forward joggle can also be used to execute repeated chords with ease, precision, and power. To do this you must master the passive finger, knuckle-dipping movement. This is often difficult to learn because it requires that students overcome their habit of reaching out with or tightening their fingers when approaching the keys; here, utter finger passivity is demanded. I recommend a detached calmness in working through this process of learning *not* to do something. Prepare the first chord in **Figure 3-2** with high wrists and with completely relaxed fingers in semiclaw position. Push to the bottom of the keys with forearms and remain there in claw position.

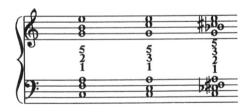

Figure 3-2. Chordal joggle action.

Alternate claw and palm positions with spaghettilike fingers whose tips stay glued to the bottom of the keys; arms travel along the trombone slide diagonal. Increase the pace, decreasing movement size; feel all tension evaporate to permit an elbow vibrato. Stop midway and allow keys to surface. Now, play the chord softly, stroking forward with utterly passive fingers that neither reach out nor tighten: fingers mold to the keys transmitting thrust through skeletal resistance alone. Gain conscious control of this resilient playing action of the finger knuckles by practicing repetitions of each chord in **Figure 3-2**, walking out chromatically for several tones; experiment with various speeds and dynamics, adding a subtle amount of graded finger tension for louder sounds. As no energy is wasted trying to "hold" the fingers, it is possible to achieve extremely fast, full, and relaxed repetitions with surprising ease. Experiment with the following examples and others you can find.

Example 3-9. The left-hand forearm joggles the repeated chords with spaghettilike fingers whose tips never leave the keys. There is complete control.

Schubert, Impromptu, Op. 90, No. 1, mm. 152–154.

Example 3-10. Execute the left-hand repeated-chord crescendo with a tightening vibrato of the elbow; the fingers remain loose and passively molded to the shape of the keys.

Schumann, *Carnaval*, "Florestan," mm. 57–63.

Example 3-11. Enjoy the booming reverberation you can generate on the repeated chords with forearms stroking behind loose, mostly passive fingers.

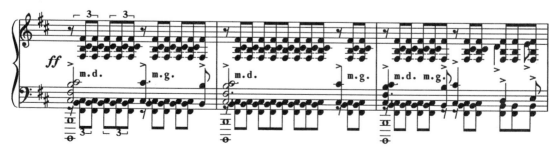

Rachmaninoff, Prelude, Op. 23, No. 21, mm. 22–24.

15 B **Forearm-Finger Grouping**

A forearm-finger grouping consists of a motivic unit of two or more notes that can be mentally linked and physically organized so that each group of several notes is played within a single forearm drop. The approach simplifies faster-moving passages and allows the groups to be rhythmically energized and renewed at will.

The first line of **Figure 3-3** (schematized for the left hand) illustrates how this technique works for a two-note group. Approach the motivic unit as a chord with fingers covering both notes. Drop 1s and 2s on the adjacent white keys with slightly lowered wrists, thumbs on octave Ds, then let 2s surface. Note and retain the resulting positional mold: drop on 1s with 2s poised to snap (the last note of the group); snap 2s, kicking the forearms slightly out of the keys and noticing that 1s overlap to release *with* 2s, not before. Ingrain the forearm-drop/finger-snap sequence in place, increasing speed to MM 100, then walk outward and return. Reverse directions, dropping on preset 2s, and snapping thumbs. In this case, preset an opposite finger mold, found by dropping on both fingers and lifting 1s to the surface. Then, drop on 2s and snap 1s for the release which, because of the thumbs' sideways movement, is more difficult.

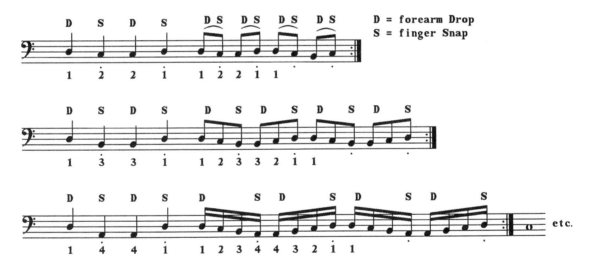

Figure 3-3. **Forearm-finger exercise pattern.**

To review the important steps of forearm-finger grouping: (a) cover all notes as though playing a chord; (b) play the first note as a forearm drop on fingers set to reach bottom as the others just touch the surface of their respective keys; (c) play the last note of the group as a finger snap which releases all the held notes, kicking the fingers and forearms out of the keys. Forearm movement (elbow hinging) is thus tied to the group's first and last notes; minimize wrist and shoulder movement so as to maintain a tight synchronicity between forearm and fingertip motion. With stable wrists, the movements can be quite quick and as small as the distance of key depth itself.

Practice other two-finger combinations, both adjacent and spread, until they become habitual in both directions. Wider intervals affect hand position and correspondence, but the forearm-finger sequence remains unchanged. Move up the scale chromatically with a given two-finger practice example in order to gain experience in accommodating your finger levels to the tier system as well as to the uneven finger mold. Practice these two finger, forearm-finger grouping movements on the following excerpts, and on others you can find.

Example 3-12. Here we have a two-note forearm-finger grouping. Practice the right hand as described above in the text, making no attempt to release the dropping finger or play the finger-snap note softer.

Beethoven, Sonata in D Minor, Op. 31, No. 2, first movement, mm. 9-12.

Example 3-13. Use forearm-finger (forearm-drop/finger-snap) action to play the passage. You can compress the two notes rhythmically ever so slightly.

Beethoven, Sonata in F♯ Major, Op. 78, second movement, mm. 20–24.

Expand to three- and four-note groupings using the formula suggested in **Figure 3-3**; play both hands in contrary motion, overlapping fingers from first to last. Note that a *D* in the figure implies a close forearm drop on a set finger, and that an *S* denotes a finger snap that kicks the forearms minimally out of the keys.

Start on octave Ds and play the complete exercise on white keys; the quarter-note movement gives you an opportunity to ingrain the alternating finger molds before the faster movement arrives. Do additional practice shifting outward for several starting notes. When completely comfortable with the arm-finger sequence, try whole tone and minor-third spacings touching near the fallboard; move outward chromatically, fingering four-note diminished groups with 5s. Concentrate on the precision of the drops, the accuracy of the finger level settings, and the crispness of the snaps. Redo the entire routine using an unfolding-finger coordination; this latter effects the hand position and finger-stroke direction, calling for finger springs (rather than finger snaps) to throw your forearms out of the keys. Compare and memorize the kinesthetic differences between the two coordinations. Try the following examples.

Example 3-14. Block the implied right-hand chords, then use forearm-finger action to play the right-hand triplets; compress each group rhythmically.

Beethoven, Variations in C Minor, Var. 19, mm. 6–7.

Example 3-15. Think and shape the right-hand thumb line, letting forearm-finger principles take care of the rest.

Chopin, Fantasy-Impromptu, mm. 15–16.

Example 3-16. The right-hand forearm drops on the quarter-note beats; the sixteenth notes are "spit" out lightly in forearm-finger groupings of four notes each. Learn the passage initially in blocked form.

Schubert, Impromptu in A♭ Major, Op. 90, No. 4, mm. 1–3.

A forearm-finger group is primarily a melodic entity, its outlines defined by skips or changes of direction. If these building modules happen to be rhythmically displaced, the basic coordination is only slightly altered. Look at some of the possibilities in **Figure 3-4**. When a forearm-finger grouping starts with a single note before the beat (A), the second note becomes its rhythmic center. Dropping fingers are set slightly closer to palm position so that the forearms can descend beyond the drop note to reach "bottom" on the sixteenth note occurring on the beat. The drop note becomes what I call a *forenote*, not an upbeat, signifying no delay and no change of arm direction leading to the beat. With two forenotes (B), the third note becomes the deepest point of penetration. In the last example (C), arms descend to the finger snap.

Figure 3-4. Rhythmically displaced forearm-finger groupings.

Experiment with various numbers of forenotes and habituate yourself to these finger positions and movements. Find passages in your music to organize in this way, using forenotes and forearm-finger principles; it will improve the accuracy and fluidity of your playing. Try the following excerpts and find other relevant examples.

Example 3-17. Organize this passage with one forenote to improve its fluidity and wider linear shape.

Beethoven, Sonata in D Minor, Op. 31, No. 2, first movement, mm. 83–87.

Example 3-18. Play each melodic grouping with two forenotes; the extended line undulates in quarters, yet still remains whole.

Chopin, Etude in C Minor, Op. 10, No. 12, mm. 5–7.

Example 3-19. With three forenotes the left-hand forearm reaches "bottom" with the last or finger-snap note of each of the groups.

Schumann, Fantasy in C Major, Op. 17, first movement, mm. 1-3.

15 C **Upper-Arm Gesturing—Cycles**

Most legato finger passages requiring speed, clarity, flexibility, and endurance are supported by arm movements that I call *gesturing*. An upper-arm gesture is a single-directional motion that underlays and sustains linear melodic movement up to five fingers. Fingers remain reasonably passive and very close as the traveling arm transfers weight from one fingertip to the next in a smooth, continuous line. An example of this movement is the quick playing of a broken chord. With experience, pianists can learn to slow and control this action and to string the continuously moving gestures together in support of the musical shapes the fingers encounter. The purpose of this section is to introduce the idea and to train you in the employ of these useful arm gestures that underlay fast, well-coordinated finger movement.

The upper arms gesture in three directions to support finger velocity: they pull with scooping hands, they pronate moving to the outside, and they push, moving forward. Pianists continuously use these movements in various combinations to support finger action. I begin with the simplest type, one-way directional movement within a single hand position. I caution you to play *pianissimo* throughout, because these exercises involve the handling of very fast notes.

With thumbs on octave Ds, scoop a 1-3-5 triad, as first described in Section 10 B, several times. Repeat the triad as a whiplike broken chord moving 1 to 5, notes releasing at the end altogether; walk laterally for several notes and return. Next, sound the same triad with a pronating gesture (with elbow movement to the outside), first as a solid chord, then as a fast broken chord (i.e., 1-3-5); repeat several times. Finally, push the triad with flattened fingers, a stroke resembling the pushing arm staccato of Section 8 B. Habituate yourself to these three upper-arm gestures in contrary motion, then repeat the entire routine (using the identical arm gestures) breaking the triads in the opposite direction (5-3-1) towards the thumbs.

Next, scoop five white notes as a chordal cluster several times. Following the process above, break the chord 1 to 5; repeat the breaking scoop gesture eight times, gradually slowing it until each note becomes a clear "moving quarter" paced slowly enough to accommodate individual correspondence adjustments. Now reverse the process, speeding the notes until the solid chord reappears. You discover that finger speed is purely a function of arm speed, and that there is little to no sense of independent individual stroking or releasing. Repeat the procedure with a pronating gesture and then, with a pushing one. Finally, again following the routine above, do all three gestures moving from 5 to 1. Gesturing enables you to spit out exceedingly fast, if soft, notes with a single swipe of the arm, and to control their tempo by adjusting your arm speed.

Practice each of the three upper-arm gestures on various five-finger patterns: spread to whole-tone clusters and five-note diminished chords; shift chromatically, playing in the black area. Note that the larger the spread of the fingers, the more pronounced the lateral element of the movement. Practice the gestures with hands together in contrary motion; try some outward movement, some inward. Then, switch to playing parallel to experience the vast difference in the inner sensations. Listen carefully for evenness of the notes as they slow up in the repeated broken chords, observing that it is largely the initial hand placement that controls and determines the success of the results.

Use the finger number patterns in **Figure 3-5** to practice gestures that include simple changes of finger direction; supply some of your own, too. After covering the notes, move arms through to the last note as though playing forenotes descending to a beat. Do white keys, then wider, more complex spreads that include black keys. Some patterns work better with one particular gesture, but for experience, do each pattern in all three directions. Do contrary and parallel practice. Work for speed and clarity, but never for volume. Pace yourself carefully to avoid becoming tense or tired; rest whenever necessary.

1-2-3-4-3	4-3-2-1-2	1-2-1-2-1	2-1-2-1-2
2-3-4-5-4	5-4-3-2-3	2-3-2-3-2	3-2-3-2-3
1-2-3-4-2	4-3-2-1-3	3-4-3-4-3	4-3-4-3-4
2-3-4-5-3	5-4-3-2-4	4-5-4-5-4	5-4-5-4-5
1-2-3-2-1	3-2-1-2-3	1-3-2-4-5	5-3-4-2-1
2-3-4-3-2	4-3-2-3-4	1-4-3-5-2	5-2-3-1-4
3-4-5-4-3	5-4-3-4-5	1-5-2-4-3	5-1-4-2-3
1-2-3-1-2	3-2-1-3-2	1-2-1-5-4	5-4-5-1-2
2-3-4-2-3	4-3-2-4-3	3-4-5-3-4	5-4-3-5-4

Figure 3-5. Arm gesture finger patterns with simple directional change.

Find passages in the literature you are studying to apply this gesturing principle. Also see the following applications.

Example 3-20. The right hand is essentially broken chords that are played as single-directional arm gestures.

Debussy, "Gardens in the Rain," mm. 1–3.

Example 3-21. These right-hand patterns change direction and notes, but with the help of the fingers, can be incorporated into a single arm gesture.

Debussy, "Reflections in the Water," mm. 20–21.

Example 3-22. The left hand plays straightforward broken-chord patterns.

Beethoven, Variations in C Minor, Var. 31, mm. 1–2.

Example 3-23. The upper-arm gestures are parallel.

Liszt, Sonata in B Minor, mm. 529–530.

Example 3-24. In this example of widespread gesturing, move both arms in the same direction.

Chopin, Etude Op. 12, No. 11, mm. 10–12.

You must learn to handle directional changes, like those recurring in repeating patterns, without sharply altering the smooth flow of the arm; cycling arms combine with fingers in ways that continue their support of the fingers and promote fluidity. See **Figure 3-6**. Most cycles progress in the pronating direction as banking arms circle forward to play the outside note and beyond, before the pulling return to the inside of the hand. Begin by playing the exercise pattern using fingers 3, 4, and 5; start low near the edge of the keys and move each hand forward with a pronating circle to touch 5s on their inside tips. Continue around playing 4s forward of their previous contact (this is important), and return. Repeat the pattern with arms circling in and out until the movements feel completely natural; the sensations resemble those of the sidesaddle playing in Section 12 E. Play even eighth notes in $\frac{2}{4}$ time to speed up the circles. Drill the movements on white keys and in the black area on whole tone patterns moving up chromatically. Repeat the entire exercise routine with the indicated alternate fingerings, 2-3-4 and 1-2-3.

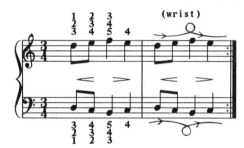

Figure 3-6. Directional changes to the outside.

The pattern in **Figure 3-7** displaces the rhythm of Figure 3-6 to focus on the inside change of direction; play first using 3-2-1 and note that the pronating circles are retained. Start the exercise with high wrists in the black area near the fallboard, pulling (falling) downward to the thumbs; again the middle finger, 2, touches in variant spots on its key. Circle the pattern until it is ingrained, then circle faster in even eighth notes on both white and whole tone patterns. Drill the alternate fingerings as well: 4-3-2 and 5-4-3. Combine **Figures 3-6 and 3-7** into a five-note circle, modifying correspondences as you move; widen the cycles to five-note diminished chords, moving up chromatically. You have now experienced how cycling arms can provide continuous, uninterrupted support to fingers covering notes that change direction.

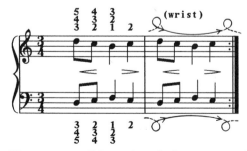

Figure 3-7. Directional changes to the inside.

Repeated broken chord patterns are executed by cycling upper arms over unfolding fingers, a movement more pronounced with wider patterns. Some typical examples are shown in **Figure 3-8.**

Figure 3-8. Broken-chord gesturing patterns.

Walk each pattern out chromatically for several notes and back, playing hands in contrary motion centered on middle D. Octave jump examples require added dexterity. The cycling-arm gestures renew the impetus and keep the rhythm moving evenly forward—all without disturbing the line. Try the following excerpts.

Example 3-25. The left arm circles quietly over the triplets to sustain the rhythmic flow.

Mozart, Sonata in F Major, K. 332, third movement, mm. 50–54.

Example 3-26. The left-hand circling movement is larger, and at the octave skip, quicker; fingers are close and reasonably passive, as the arm takes the lead.

Beethoven, Sonata in E Major, Op. 14, No. 1, first movement, mm. 69–71.

Example 3-27. The left arm moves continually in pushing-pronating circles. This kind of circular accompaniment provides the harmony and rhythmic impetus.

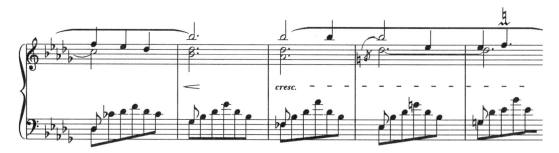

Chopin, Scherzo in B♭ Minor, Op. 31, mm. 202–206.

Example 3-28. Arms actively gesture each quintuplet providing impetus, sonority, and excitement.

Beethoven, Sonata in F Minor, Op. 57, first movement, mm. 84–85.

Related arm cycles can also be used to support trills and tremolos; see the instructions pertaining to hand bounces in Section 10 A. Just as bouncing hands can be incorporated within a pull/push arm cycle, so can trills and tremolos. Experience this by executing two or three trill alternations with pulling arms, then a like number with pushing arms. Note how fingers slide back and forth along the keys, and how much increased impetus and endurance is created as a result of the arm-finger combination. Make up exercises to ingrain this coordination.

15 D Finger Length Adaptations

It is advantageous for pianists, whenever possible, to maintain their hands in a natural semicurved position in which the longer middle fingers play in front of the shorter outside ones. Ideally, all fingers should learn to cope with the uneven heights and close quarters of the black area in order to keep the hands in their strongest, most natural, most relaxed configuration. Once in a while, however, in legato playing, intractable logistical problems do force the fingers to make special *length adaptations*. The purpose of this section is to present some of the possibilities the fingers have for dealing with these topographically awkward situations.

Begin the length adaptation exercise by placing the fingertips on adjacent white keys in the gray area of the keyboard with thumbs on octave Ds. With still arms, set up a slow legato alternation between fingers 5 and 3, playing every other 5 on the black key to the outside (RH 5 alternates A and A♯, LH 5 alternates G and G♭): flatten 5s to reach the black keys, recurve them to play the original white keys. Next, continue the slow tremolo to shift 3s chromatically in the same manner (RH 3 alternates F and F♯, LH 3 alternates B and B♭) while 5s remain playing their original white keys. Note that fingers alone make these length adjustments. Repeat the exercise using 4s and 2s, then 3s and 1s, picking the closest black key as the alternate note for the active, length-adjusting finger. Perform these slow, mirrored tremolos one pair of fingers at a time. Recall a related instance of changing the shape of a stroking finger in Section 12 E, two-finger sidesaddle walking.

When you feel at ease with these adaptation movements, play a series of simultaneous major seconds walking out chromatically, touching only in the gray area; make all necessary in/out adjustments with fingers alone, none with the hands, wrists, or arms. Try this with various adjacent finger combinations, then perform simultaneously sounding thirds moving outward chromatically with varied relevant fingers. Experiment also with different chordal spacings and positions to see how and where these finger-shape manipulations might be usefully applied.

Another finger length adaptation is a rare, specialized coordination I call the *pulling midjoint touch*. Place 1s and 5s in the white area on the bottom of white-key fifths, 1s on octave Ds. Sound the three longer, middle fingers together by actively flexing their midjoints; nail joints, remaining passive, bend backwards as the two outer phalanxes of the fingers slide under. The knuckles, though supporting the action, barely move. Note that the midjoint movement here is opposite to that in the unfolding finger coordination, during which midjoints extend rather than flex. This strange coordination (which feels like walking on shortened legs) serves two purposes: it can relieve long muscle tension, even in scale playing, for it is a looser than ordinary pulling touch; and it allows longer fingers to play without raising the arch beyond the reach of the shorter, outside fingers.

Apply this coordination and positioning to spread chords in the black area. For instance, play diminished-seventh chords moving out chromatically by squeezing middle-finger midjoints under; experience the secure, squeezing key contact. Open the seventh chords, playing one note at a time, to see how relaxed this flexing midjoint touch can feel.

You can combine these two adaptations by holding notes with a short-legged middle finger in the gray area of the keyboard while straightening (lengthening) or curving other fingers to help them reach their keys. Find additional uses for these unusual finger manipulations.

Section 16 **Lateral Movements**

This section focuses upon concepts and movements involving shifts of the arms sideways at the keyboard and upon the accomplishment of such shifts with speed and accuracy. Keep in mind that every time you approach the instrument you must meticulously center yourself and stabilize your body against the uncentering thrusts of large, quick lateral arm movements. Also remember that you must release your shoulders to the outside so your arms can move freely in any direction. Most length-adjusting movements of the arms are initiated by the shoulder girdle, the first link in the piano-playing chain: small movements of the shoulder girdle produce amplified movements of the hands because of the levering length of the arms.

16 A **Lateral Extension—Preparation Shifts**

Lateral speed and accuracy are learned skills; the following basic exercises are designed to achieve these skills. After carefully centering yourself, play the notes in **Figure 3-9** with right hand alone. Use the figure-eight motion of PM 6 to extend each interval one key until you reach three-octave D; then, return to your starting position. The arm weaves continuously, doing pronating circles to play 1s, supinating circles to play 5s. Upper arms lead the motion in both the outward and inward directions. Do the mirror image of this exercise with your left hand, spending more time on the weaker or less accurate side. Experiment (again one hand at a time) with extending the notes chromatically, concentrating on accuracy and on the additional problem of playing black keys. When you become reasonably accurate and comfortable, play the exercise considerably faster using a pull/push single-circle arm pattern, pulling 1s and pushing 5s. The faster you play, the more you must loosely "throw" your hand and "believe" that it is the hand that pulls the arms.

Figure 3-9. Lateral figure-eight exercise pattern.

Perform the notes in **Figure 3-10** with a right arm figure-eight movement; spread to four octaves and return; the upper arm leads a relaxed limb with loose, straightened fingers. Move without hesitation; it is better to miss an occasional note while maintaining a smooth motion than to prepare any particular shift jerkily. If initially you find it difficult to make the large, smooth maneuvers, do not become discouraged; loose shoulders, arms, and fingers, faithful practice, and positive thinking pay dividends. Do a mirror-image pattern with your left hand, and spend more time on the weaker or less well-coordinated arm. Work to increase speed, accuracy, and range. Try other finger combinations and invent similar exercises on your own. Begin to "throw" your hand when the tempo or distance makes this necessary.

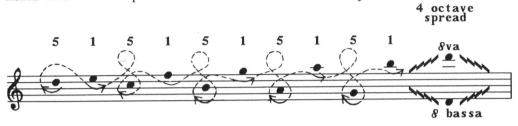

Figure 3-10. Doubly extending lateral exercise pattern.

There is a procedure for learning large, quick, lateral shifts that do not form part of a regular pattern. I call these *preparation shifts*. This advantageous practice routine prepares you for the myriad small and large arm and hand shifts that occur regularly in ordinary playing.

Begin by touching your right-hand thumb on middle D; play it sharply, throwing your thumb quickly to the surface of octave D; the thumb lands on but does not play octave D. Pause to calculate any needed adjustments. Repeat the spaced practice shots—these aim-and-throw ballistic shifts with their exact lateral distance—until they become an integral part of the first note's playing impulse and psychologically quite separate from the sounding of the landing note. The landing note, when finally played, sets off its own forward-looking shift when needed.

Preparation practice is extremely efficient for learning quick, single, lateral gestures. Rehearse a left-hand equivalent of the above octave shift. Then, accustom yourself to a two-octave jump in each hand. Try both distances, one hand at a time, playing a 1-3-5 triad. Note that the larger the jump, the more the figure-eight adjustments come into play.

When the shift involves a hand shape change as well, ingrain this first, before turning to deal with the lateral movement. Practice with your right hand, for example, the preparation shift in **Figure 3-11,** which shows the steps one takes to learn a shift moving from a three- to a four-note triad while also jumping two octaves. Proceed as follows: (a) habituate yourself to shifting the hand from the three- to four-note form of the chord in place; (b) ingrain the two-octave jump with thumb alone; and (c) combine these two elements, all without playing the landing note(s). Notice how the very silence created by preparing but not playing the landing note(s) binds the shift to the previous playing impulse, and separates both from the new sound. **Example 3-29** exhibits a dramatic use of this concept.

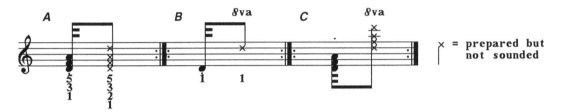

Figure 3-11. Preparation shifts.

Example 3-29. Practice first the shift from smaller hand position to octave with the thumbs remaining in place, then practice the lateral thumb shifts alone before combining the two. Prepare the take-off notes and, while practicing, touch but do not sound the landing notes.

Schumann, Fantasy in C Major, Op. 17, second movement (coda), mm. 251–253.

16 B Walking Rebounds—Parallel Motion—Octaves

In Section 9 C you learned to perform a controlled number of repetitions of a note, interval, or chord generated by a single forearm gravity drop. The power and ease afforded by this coordination may be extended to play repeated sounds that also move laterally. For example, practice the right-hand patterns indicated in **Figure 3-12** with 1s and 5s in resting position; play in contrary motion using a forearm stroke with high wrists. Begin **Figure 3-12A** at MM 60, gradually increasing the tempo to MM 88; walk the pattern outward for a few keys, and then return. Relax during the rests; if necessary, extend them, to avoid any build-up of tension or fatigue. Keep arms, hands, and fingers as loose as practicable, and insure that the impetus of the initial drop generates each separate group in its entirety.

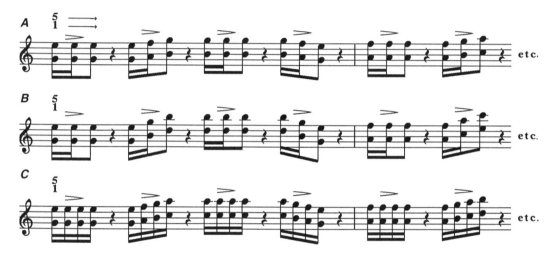

Figure 3-12. Walking rebounds.

Figure 3-12B provides practice in speeding and enlarging the lateral movement. Walk this pattern outward for several keys to ingrain the movement. The pattern in **Figure 3-12C** asks you to increase the number of rebounds to three (four sounds in all) while simultaneously performing the lateral movement. Next, perform all three patterns at faster speeds up to MM 116, this time using a hand-bounce coordination. Contrast and memorize the difference in sound and kinesthetic feel between the two coordinations.

Bind forearm rebounding groups together to form a series of mirrored, *continuity impulses* as shown in **Figure 3-13A** and **B**. Begin the exercise at MM 60 and increase the tempo to MM 80, resting at the half notes. Play accurately but softly and loosely, like a rag doll, pacing yourself to avoid a build-up of tension or fatigue. Decrease the size of the movements to increase speed. Within these parameters work for continuity, quickness, and sustaining ability. Reduce long notes to quarters, then in time eliminate them. Notice that it is your elbows that create the vertical forearm movement while your upper arms, moving in loose shoulders, create the lateral movement. Perform both lines in **Figure 3-13** using the hand bounce, experiencing and noting the difference in sound and feel between the two coordinations. Increase speed and lightness to a quarter equals MM 92.

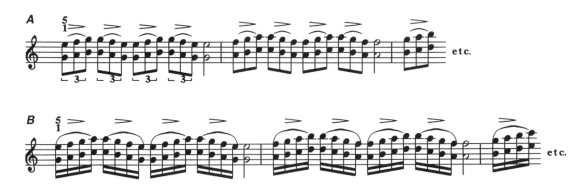

Figure 3-13. Rebound continuity practice routine.

Apply these principles to the following musical excerpts. Decide in a particular situation whether the forearm or the hand repetition is preferable.

Example 3-30. Play the groups of three right-hand octaves within one forearm rebounding impulse, but with an awareness of the two-bar melodic shape.

Beethoven, 32 Variations in C Minor, Var. 16, mm. 1-3.

Example 3-31. Use forearms for power, renewing the impulse every beat.

Beethoven, Sonata in F Major, Op. 54, first movement, mm. 25–28.

Example 3-32. Bounce your right hand with wrist held high, renewing the arm impulse every three chords.

Beethoven, Sonata in C Major, Op. 2, No. 3, fourth movement, mm. 1–6.

Parallel Motion. Until now I have emphasized contrary motion almost exclusively in these exercises because its basic simplicity centers your body and fosters equal development of your right and left sides; it prompts your arms, hands, and fingers to do the same things simultaneously, to reach out and back together, to pronate or supinate together. Parallel movement radically alters this state of affairs because it lacks any such uniformity. For example, to direct both arms right, shoulders perform reverse operations; right hand pronation is matched with left hand supination, right hand adduction with left hand abduction, and so on. Take a moment to picture these contrasting, non-centering phenomena. Stand up and perform the contrary movements of the last several exercises in the air in a parallel mode, "listening" to your muscles make the necessary adjustments.

Return to Section 4, IM 2, to redo the exercise integrating fingers and hands with rotating arms on a flat surface (presented in Figure 1-21A and B). Return also to Section 2, PM 6, to redo the lateral-arm figure-eight drill. Both of these primary integrational exercises were set forth originally in contrary motion. Take the time now to experience these motions moving parallel. Realize the following: contrary motion directs your body's responses to be alike on both sides; parallel motion forces the two sides of your body to make opposite responses. Carefully digest these new sensations. In learning to coordinate parallel actions, it sometimes helps to imagine your third finger knuckles joined with a sturdy, invisible tie that obliges your two sides to move equidistantly parallel while performing the opposing coordinations simultaneously. The entire body must react to counterbalance these destabilizing forces.

After gaining control of the two integrative exercises mentioned above in the parallel, as well as contrary mode, rework the forearm exercises **(Figs. 3-12** and **3-13)**: sound right hand as written, but play your left hand two octaves below and parallel. As before begin slowly and increase speed gradually; alternate parallel and contrary practice until you gain mental and physical control over the two very different situations and sensations.

The virtuoso literature is full of parallel movement, as composers routinely add weight to single line gestures. Scales, double octaves, and parallel chords abound. Coordinations once learned bilaterally must now be integrated with their opposites. When confronted with such challenges, learn the movements one side at a time before thoughtfully combining the two sides. Legato passages are particularly troublesome and should be carefully fingered to keep your hands shifting together. Also, the modifications demanded of the fingers in adjusting to the two-tier system present additional complexities. But once again, to pinpoint a problem, even an extremely difficult one, is to move towards a solution.

Octaves. Cover white-key sixths with claw 1s and 5s, palm bones back, middle fingers out front, thumbs on octave Ds. Drop forearms in place, snapping fingers at the bottom: 1s pull across the keys, 5s flex more or less in line with the keys. Walk outward and back experimenting with dynamics, dropping heights and tempo. Practice an equal amount of parallel motion, further ingraining the deft grasping movement with its subtle timing. Compare this with the high-wrist position learned in Section 11 A, a similar coordination, but with palm thumbs on their heads. Alternate high and low wrist positions and imprint the differences. Return to claw position and expand the sixths to octaves: extend thumb midjoints, abduct your hands, pronate your arms, and lower your arches. Practice both contrary and parallel patterns to habituate yourself to the octave-grasping motion; adjust wrists laterally to keep fingers landing in the gray area.

Execute parallel double octaves spaced an octave apart. Bounce forearms with firmed wrists and snapping fingers. Press 2s and 3s together (try one or the other on top) to help stabilize the hand. Play lightly and at moderate speed, imagining a spacing bar between third finger knuckles; do white-key, chromatic, and whole-tone scales, as well as diminished, major, and minor arpeggios. Set up zigzag patterns that involve skips and changes of direction; play in the gray area to minimize in/out movement; be prepared to adjust legs and torso to maintain overall balance, and carefully pace yourself so as not to build up tension or fatigue.

Practice octaves in assorted ways: with thumbs only, with 5s only, and with each thumb combined with the other hand's fifth finger. It pays to gain considerable skill in double-octave playing. Do similar exercises using the hand-bounce coordination to experience the lightness and increased speeds now possible. To assist velocity, fingers make tiny grasping movements with each landing. Alternate forearm and hand touches to gain control of both. Work for accuracy and fluency. Try the following forearm-octave examples.

Example 3-33. Use forearm drops and rebounds for power, with the major impulse on the first beat of each measure; finger all octaves with 5s; rebound the single eighth note.

Chopin, Scherzo in C♯ Minor, Op. 39, mm. 367–376.

Example 3-34. These octaves are powerful, but shaped and expressive; you may want to finger some of them.

Schubert, Impromptu, Op. 142, No. 1, mm. 40–43.

Example 3-35. Use forearms, imagining an invisible spacing bar locking your hands a given distance apart; play all octaves with grasping 1s and 5s landing in the gray area.

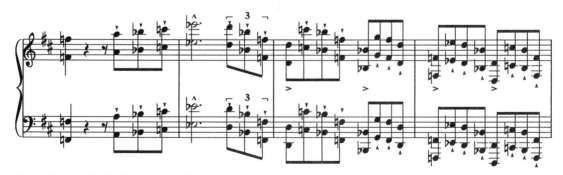

Liszt, Sonata in B Minor, mm. 57–60.

16 C **Fake Legato**

I use the term *fake legato* to cover a complex of special technical applications necessary for performing extended, quickly moving, lateral legato lines. The rubric of fake legato incorporates three separate elements: (1) continuity of linear expression beyond the reach of one hand position; (2) special handling of shift and landing notes; and (3) seamless handling of the directional changes at either end.

Work with the generic exercise pattern in **Figure 3-14**. Drop your right forearm on a set thumb as though beginning a forearm-finger grouping. The third finger, which touches the surface of its key, executes a finger snap that kicks the arms loosely to the new position; fingers 1 and 3 retain a constant spacing. The relaxed landing note should be softer than the preceding finger-snap (take-off) note. At the top of the four-note pattern, the first of the repeated notes is snapped while the second is played forward with straightened finger as part of the larger arm cycle. Returning, the snapping (and flexing) thumb propels the arm to the inside, while the bottom (finger-arm) double thumb combination blends with the pulling portion of the arm cycle.

Repeat this series of steps until all "bumps" disappear and a uniform line moves effortlessly within a flowing cycle. The active snaps speed the arm shifts and help dynamically to cover the breaks; the soft landings prevent accents. Rhythmically, it is counter-productive to play the preshift note early, in the hope of creating additional time for the shift; in fact, the opposite occurs—the later the snapped note sounds, the more psychological time there is for the shift. Help to consolidate the separate arm shifts into a larger linear gesture by performing a crescendo or rubato spanning the complete eight-note shape. Accustom yourself to the entire sequence of right-hand motions for **Figure 3-14A** and **B**, and learn a mirror equivalent for the left hand. Practice hands together, first in contrary motion, then in parallel motion an octave apart. Note the differences.

Figure 3-14. Fake-legato exercise pattern.

Extend the pattern as suggested in **Figure 3-15**; then use this extension idea as the basis for practicing the movements, intervals, fingering, and ranges outlined in **Figure 3-16**. Begin with each hand alone (left hand doing the mirror image), then play both hands together in contrary and parallel modes. Note that fast scale playing requires fake-legato arm shifts of thirds and fourths and that fast arpeggios call for fake-legato arm shifts of an octave.

Figure 3-15. Fake-legato exercise routine—extended lateral range.

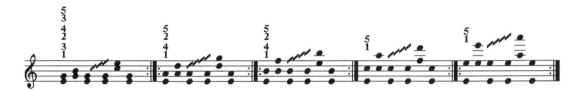

Figure 3-16. Fake-legato exercise routine—extended interval and lateral range.

Practice the suggested patterns in **Figure 3-17** using a similar format. The literature often demands the combining of various broken chords with shifting or cycling arms to create flowing, extended lines. These exercises prepare you for this challenge. Try your newly acquired skills on the examples below.

Figure 3-17. Fake-legato exercise routine—chordal practice patterns.

Example 3-36. These right-hand sextolets must flow smoothly without hesitation, undulating twice a measure.

Chopin, Ballade in A♭ Major, No. 3, mm. 170–172.

Example 3-37. Fake-legato shifts make the continuous three-octave line possible.

Chopin, Etude, Op. 25, No. 12, mm. 1–2.

Example 3-38. The left hand remains open to an octave span for the entire passage; the fake-legato shifts require finger snaps and lateral arm shifts.

Brahms, Capriccio, Op. 116, No. 3, mm. 80–82.

Example 3-39. The right hand stays comfortably extended throughout without concern for physical connection; the lateral movement is accomplished by arm shifts using fake-legato concepts; the goal is an extended, undivided line.

Chopin, Ballade in G Minor, Op. 23, mm. 47–49.

Section 17 Release Movements

This section is concerned with the varied lengths of notes played without pedal, their qualities of sound, and the manner in which hands and fingers physically release their keys. For example, following a forearm drop, hands are able to release in both directions: flexing under or extending forward. In the case of the hand-finger staccato, bouncing hands combine with snapping fingers to create a unity of intention such that neither movement is primary. Finally, we shall see how pure finger releases can add great variety and subtlety to your playing.

17 A Hand Releases

Drop your forearms on white-key sixths with 1s and 5s in resting position, thumbs on octave Ds. Pause, then extend your wrists: fingertips slide forward and arc upwards. Retract forearms and relax wrists to prepare the next drop. Gradually decrease the stay at the bottom until you find yourself playing extremely short staccatos. Ingrain the hand-extension releases in place before walking outward for a few keys and returning; do some parallel practice as well. Experiment with varying dynamics, tempos, and dropping heights. Try one or two brutally loud "shots" which, because of their shortness, can be harsh and ugly, and must be prudently monitored. Pace yourself so as not to build up any fatigue or tension.

You can release your hands in the scooping direction as well, sending wrists upward. This coordination assumes a position that is closely related to the high wrist upper-arm gravity drop of Section 8 C. It too is capable of huge sonorities, which must be monitored for sound quality. Alternate releases to experience a push/pull arm cycle: extension releases mesh with pushing arms, as scooping releases fit with pulling arm strokes; alternating the two increases the potential for speed.

Use hand releases for short, sharp, individual notes or chords. These can be played as softly as you like, but if you decide to use the full power of the forearms, be careful that the quickness of the hand releases does not produce indeterminate pitches or ugly, repellent sounds; and also that the strength of the forearms does not overwhelm and fatigue the weaker hand muscles. Be observant; and judiciously pace your efforts to avoid tension and fatigue.

17 B Hand-Finger Staccato

Hands and fingers can be combined in such a way that the hands, swinging in the wrists, back individual snapping fingers. The result is a highly efficient, clearly articulated finger staccato. Hands are capable of bouncing about four times to each MM 92; these repetitions may be used to support successive fingers in nonlegato progressions.

Cover white keys, thumbs on octave Ds. Lightly bounce four times on each finger at MM 72; move in contrary motion from 1s to 5s and back. Next, bounce once on each finger at the same tempo. Circle the pattern several times and move outward for several notes before returning. Contrast these staccatos produced by pulling fingers with those accomplished by unfolding ones; with the former, wrists may be low or high, fingers less curved, and there is scoop pressure; in the latter, wrists tend to be average or higher, fingers become claw-shaped, and there is less pronation. Become aware of the different tone qualities the two coordinations create. Try the above routines moving parallel, two octaves apart, following first the right hand, then left hand direction. Practice separately before habituating yourself to hands together, and note the contrasting kinesthetic sensations associated with contrary and parallel movement.

Play whole-tone and minor-third spacings in the black key area. Notice how wider stretches require straighter fingers and larger correspondence adjustments. Perform with pulling and unfolding fingers in combination with the bouncing hands, in contrary and parallel directions. Increase speed gradually until you can comfortably perform all varieties of hand-finger staccatos at about four bounces to MM 92. Try this coordination on the following examples.

Example 3-40. The hand bounces with each right-hand finger snap as the arm shapes the melodic line.

Schumann, "Catch Me," mm. 1–4.

Example 3-41. Hands and fingers work together to produce a soft, exciting, highly articulated sonority.

Liszt, Sonata in B Minor (middle section), mm. 466–470.

Example 3-42. Left-hand fingers snap in combination with the bouncing hand.

Beethoven, Sonata in D Major, Op. 28, second movement, mm. 1–5.

Example 3-43. Great speed and brilliance are possible using the hand-finger staccato coordination.

Schumann, *Carnaval,* "Pantalon et Colombine," mm. 1–4.

17 C **Finger Releases**

I have demonstrated that there are a variety of ways in which to propel the finger into the key; the various strokes relate not only to the configuration of the hand before the stroke, but also to the desired musical effect. Balancing this, there is a comparable variety of ways to lift the finger which also vary with the physical and musical orientation of the moment. This section concerns itself with these latter matters.

The ability to control the timing and speed of finger releases vastly increases your potential for tonal variety. Legato implies the holding of notes long enough to insure continuity of sound, but this in itself is only part of the consideration. Pianists can vary releases along a continuum. For example, they often overlap fingers (finger pedaling) as a subtle means of enriching the sonority. At other times they deliberately lighten the sonority to let air between even quickly moving sounds. This is accomplished with close, snapping fingers backed by quiet, gently scooping hands with high wrists; the resulting sonority is softer, quicker, and more sensitive than that possible with bouncing hands. Experiment with some light, nonlegato scales or other linear passages to experience the variety of connections (or nonconnections) possible with snapping releases accomplished with fingers alone. Allow the nonlegato touch to gracefully emerge from a pulling legato, and note the qualities of sound that are created along the way.

At certain rare times, the need for speed and clarity in a non-pedaled, pure legato sonority requires that unfolding fingers be "hyper-released," or lifted quickly with extreme precision. This highly specialized *quick-release touch* is used to produce the rare and extraordinarily beautiful, fingered glissando, but its mastery will prove useful as well in a variety of other contexts. The following exercises are designed to help you develop better control of your unfolding-finger releases.

Touch the surfaces of adjacent white keys with hands in claw position, thumbs on octave Ds. Play both thumbs softly, making sounds as short as possible; the playing movement seems slower than the releasing one, which is a precisely timed, microsecond impulse raising the fingers just enough to stop the sound. One "throws" rather than presses the prepared thumbs to speed these releases, which never lift beyond the surface level of the other fingers. Pause momentarily after each thumb stroke to relax completely. Do hyper-released strokes several times on each of the other finger sets in correct correspondence and with ample spacing between sounds. The releasing fingers assume an even more curved position than that with which they started. Concentrate on the timing of the finger's directional change as it relates to a given piano's depth of action. Of course, the damper pedal remains unengaged.

Perform repeated light forearm drops playing 1s and 2s together with a relatively high arch; hyper-release first one finger than the other. Next, play exaggeratedly slow legato trills between 1s and 2s using an appropriate quick release; concentrate on the rapidly crossing fingers, the immediate relaxation, and the constant key contact. There is little sensation of downward pressure, rather a feeling of suspended buoyancy. Ingrain a slow trill, relaxing between "staccato" releases; then move directly to a fast trill, trilling as quickly and lightly as possible; gradual increases of speed are useless in this drill.

Apply the same slow/fast routine to other trilling finger pairs. I caution you to practice these releases sparingly and with as much time between releases as necessary to avoid a build-up of tension or fatigue in your finger extensor muscles. Allow all other fingers on the lifting side of the trill to move freely with the active finger. Thus, for example, in the slow practice of a trill between 3s and 4s, 5s will move with 4s, 2s will move with 3s. When ready, progress immediately to the fast trill. Soon your hands and fingers will feel light and twittery, primed for silvery glissandolike sonorities.

Circle a 1-to-5 pattern slowly, using the quick release touch; then circle the pattern quickly with proper correspondences. The sensation is that of peeling the hand back one finger at a time with no sense of downward exertion at all. Note that clarity in high-speed legato playing is as much a function of the precision of the releases as of accurate key depressions; fourth fingers in particular, and often thumbs, are prone to lazy lifting; give these weaker lifting fingers extra attention.

Apply this coordination with its prepared, slow/fast practice routine to passages you wish ultimately to sound soft, limpid, rapid, and legato, like a controlled glissando. Though rarely used in its pure form, the ability to perform this coordination gives you better conscious control of all your other finger releases. Try the quick-release touch on the following examples.

Example 3-44. The quick-release finger touch is ideal for this type of rapid, dying-away effect.

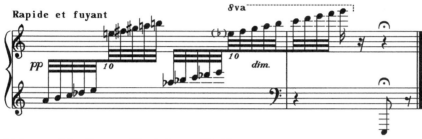

Debussy, "The Dance of Puck," mm. 95–96.

Example 3-45. This soft, clear, limpid line is a natural place to employ the quick-release finger legato.

Liszt, Sonata in B Minor, m. 200.

Section 18 **Summary**

Part Three, organized around practical pianistic concerns, encourages an efficacious consolidation of technical components. In the fusing of arms, hands, fingers, and mind into a gracefully functioning whole, be particularly wary of unintended isometric clashes, where one part of the playing mechanism, in effect, fights or cancels the efforts of another. More and more the separate elements of technique coalesce to form a coherent, harmonious whole, one that is natural, automatic, and trustworthy. At this point, a pianist can focus complete attention on purely musical matters, comfortable in the knowledge that inner hearing and musical imagination will not be needlessly compromised.

Joggle movement integrates arms with loose fingers to produce a sensitive and powerful means of playing legato up to moderate speeds and, in progressively geared relationships, beyond. Wrists provide much of the resilience that cushions shock to both the instrument and the playing apparatus. Functioning as pneumatic gears, they critically transmit upper arm energy from the shoulders through the fingertips to the keyboard.

Forearms and upper arms maneuver to support, shape, and sustain the vast panoply of finger patterns. They also blend their respective rebounding and lateral skills to open up virtuoso movement possibilities in both contrary and parallel directions. Hands and fingers join to create varied and discriminating nonlegato sonorities; both hands and fingers can individually release with extreme sharpness when necessary.

Upper arms and shoulder girdle, the prime movers of a masterful technique, apply their lateral, cycling, and repetitive movements to support the rest of the playing apparatus. They gesture, undulate, and weave to assist the fingers in creating flowing, extended musical lines, and they pulsate renewals of energy that propel the mechanism and the very music forward.

Conclusion

You have been through a process of training your mind to develop and control your body; your skill can now be applied to the performance of specific works of music. All music making requires physical effort to activate the instrument and to unite technical and aesthetic elements together into a musical actuality. Performers and listeners both respond with particular depth to the emotional power of this unity because they take place as genuine human experiences in real time.

This specialized athleticism makes us in effect dancers of the keyboard. Nothing happens until we move; nothing worthwhile happens until we move with musical purpose! The requisite physicality must be carefully nurtured, all the more so because the relative awkwardness of the demands upon the body, the beguiling intensity of musical involvement, and the pressures inherent in the act of performance, often lead to slipshod, even injurious habit patterns. The nurturing should begin as early as possible with the careful establishment of an easy, natural, well-coordinated approach to simple sound production. As tonal relationships become more sophisticated, so too will our technical movements. Maturation proceeds organically, the unconscious fruit of normal, if imaginative, effort. Physical awareness and kinesthetic insight are essential for accomplishing this.

With a prudent grounding in coordinated movement and with a critical awareness of what this means personally, even intermediate students can be safely challenged with literature that stretches them physically and musically. Ideal growth takes place when the intellectual, physical, aural, and musical keep apace. Shaping a phrase beautifully depends not only on a maturing conceptual understanding, but also on the physical ability to bring it off. Movement is so intrinsic to both technique and interpretation in music making that the inability to move with grace, elegance, and expressiveness presents a serious handicap. As pianists we essentially choreograph an evolving aesthetic ideal, aware that our musical insights and inner hearing guide the movements that give birth to the music's emotional power and meaning. In this exhilarating experience of creation lies the joy of making music, in practice and in performance.

Glossary

Abduction. Motion of the arm or hand outwards laterally from an imaginary, vertical central line.

Adduction. Motion of the arm or hand inwards laterally towards an imaginary, vertical central line.

Arch level. The distance between the knuckle level of the hand and the fingertips: a high arch indicates palm position of the hand; a low arch, claw or extended position.

Arm cycling. The recurring movement pattern of the arms as used to initiate or support key-playing action.

Arm extension with pronation. A primary movement pattern in which loosely hanging arms extend towards the floor and at the same time turn inward (pronate).

Arm flaps. Lateral movements of the upper arms: elbows go out sideways from the body and return.

Arm pulsations. The speeding up of movement within an arm cycle that occurs during key depression: it is preceded by preparatory movement and succeeded by follow-through movement.

Bilaterally symmetrical. Having the two sides of the body in a mirrored relationship that is fundamentally balanced.

Biomechanics. The study of human movement patterns.

Black area. The back two-thirds of the keyboard, including the black keys and the narrow part of the white ones.

Claw position. The position of the hand in which the first phalanx of the fingers forms a straight line with the hand at the knuckle, while the two outer phalanxes (the mid- and nail phalanxes) are highly flexed (tucked under).

Claw thumbs. The placement of the thumbs (in claw position) with their palm bones out and back creating a wide, flat palm; the second and third phalanxes of the thumbs are curved or flexed.

Clustering routine. A way of practicing to increase speed. Smaller groups of notes are forged together into larger units allowing the mind to work slower even though the notes and playing mechanism move faster: a mental change of gears.

Continuity impulse. A series of forearm rebounding drops strung together so as to create a pulsated, uninterrupted movement of tones.

Correspondence. The alignment of various parts of the playing mechanism in their strongest and most efficient relationship.

Damper pedal. The right-hand pedal which, when depressed, raises the entire bank of dampers allowing all strings to vibrate freely.

Engagement point. That point in the pedal stroke where the dampers actually leave their strings; the pedal mechanism provides free play on either side of this location.

Extended position. The position of the hand in which the palm is flat and the fingers are extended straight out.

Fake legato. A way of laterally shifting the arms and fingers so as to minimize any breaks in the smooth flow of the notes.

Fallboard. The vertical board at the back of the keyboard which hinges forward to cover the keys and become its lid.

Figure-eight movement. The graceful outward and inward lateral movement of the arms and hands which is led in both directions by the upper arms; forearms and hands elastically follow. Additional wrist and pronational arm adjustments keep the knuckle line of the hands level with the keyboard and parallel to the fallboard.

Finger length adjustment. Changing the shape (extending or curving) of the finger in order to reach a key in an awkward configuration of tones.

Finger mold. Prepositioning of the fingers in the air to fit the shape demanded by the next configuration of keys.

Finger snap. A pulling-finger coordination in which the finger, starting from a reasonably extended position, slides quickly under the palm along the key to both sound and release its key.

Finger spring. A quick unfolding finger action that kicks the forearms away from the keys.

Flexion. Muscles acting on a member in such a way as to diminish the angle on the underside of its joint.

Forearm bounce. A coordination involving bouncing forearms that hinge in the elbows while the hand and fingers remain set to move with the forearms.

Forearm drop. Forearms, with a largely gravitational movement in the elbows, approach the keyboard on a forward-diagonal line. Hands and fingers remain still, forming a unit with the forearms.

Forearm-finger grouping. A short melodic entity, the first note of which is played as a forearm drop on a set finger, while the last note of the group is played as a finger snap.

Forearm push stroke. A primary movement in which unfolding arms push the hands into the keys on a trombone-slide diagonal; forearms, moving in the elbows, are supported by forward upper-arm movement as well.

Forenotes. Those notes in a forearm-finger grouping that appear before the beat; they are played so as to avoid a change of arm direction in approaching the beat.

Gesturing. Upper-arm gestures in support of fast finger patterns; weight transfer is central to this action.

Grasping stroke. A staccato (finger-snap) stroke used by the thumb in conjunction with another flexing finger, usually at the bottom of a forearm drop: fingertips move towards each other.

Gray area. An imaginary one-inch wide lateral band that evenly overlaps the border between the black and white areas of the keyboard.

Half-octave G♯. The G♯s one-half octave to either side of middle D.

Hand bounce touch. A coordination calling for the hands to bounce up and down at the wrist to produce repeated sounds.

Hand-finger staccato. A coordination meshing bouncing hands with snapping fingers.

Hand flexion. Pulling the hand under at the wrist; the angle under the wrist decreases.

Hand hop. The final quick hand motion that is part of the pulling legato touch, which keeps the break between tones to a minimum.

Hand scoop. A coordination in which the hands pull under (flex) at the wrists while fingers remain set.

Hand scoop pressure. A sustained gentle pressure created by scooping hands and pulling arms.

Hand vocabulary. An exact equivalency between fingering and intervals; it does not change when confronted with the complicating spatial relationships of the two-tier system.

Glossary

Integrative movements. Motion patterns involving combinations of separate primary movements that are used regularly in normal playing.

Isometric training. The pitting of one set of muscles against another for the purpose of exercising both.

Joggle movement. The relaxed, controlled, sophisticated movement of the arms that backs both individual or grouped finger movements and which facilitates legato control and strength.

Karate position. A supinated position of the extended hand in which the outsides of the hands (fifth fingers on their sides) play the keys; other fingers relax to touch each other.

Kinesthetic. Having to do with the inner sensations of movement.

Knuckle joint. The joint attaching the finger to the hand.

Legato pedal. A pedal coordination that produces smooth connections between sounds even when finger connections are impossible. The pedal containing the old sonority is released to exactly match the playing of the new tones; a series of such connections creates an extended legato.

Long finger muscles. The finger muscles located in the forearms that control the outer two phalanxes of the fingers; their tendons pass through the wrists.

Middle D. The geographic center of the keyboard in the sense that lateral, spatial, and color relationships to either side of middle D are in exact mirror positions.

Midjoint. The joint between the first and second phalanxes of the finger.

Nail joint. The joint between the second and third phalanxes of the finger.

Octave D. The two Ds one octave on either side of middle D.

One and a half-octave G♯. The second G♯ on either side of middle D.

Palm knuckle joint. The primary attachment of the thumbs to the hands near the underside of the wrist.

Palm position. The position of the hand in which the first phalanxes of the fingers are as close to a right angle with the hand as possible; the tips of the fingers group into a rounded cluster. This position represents the directional goal of most finger strokes.

Pendulum swing. A primary exercise of the arms in which both arms (as single units) swing loosely in the shoulder like a pendulum, with the pulling action primary; passive movement is created in the shoulder girdle.

Phalanxes. The bones of the fingers; the first phalanx is the finger bone nearest the hand. Count outwards for the second and third phalanxes (also called the mid- and nail phalanxes).

Postural alignment. The creation of a structural entity of the torso, neck, and head; it reaches upward as the shoulder girdle releases downward to the outside.

Preparation shifts. A physical and psychological practice technique for quick, wide skips which fuses the lateral movement to the playing of the first note and separates it from the playing of the second. The practice routine calls for repeatedly jumping to the second note without sounding it.

Primary movements. The ten fundamental, abstracted movements of various parts of the playing mechanism that make up the essential building blocks of piano-playing motion.

Pronation. Twisting the arm inwards in the direction of the thumb.

Pronating circles (cycles) Recurring cycles in which the elbows move outward immediately after key depression.

Pronation extension. A primary movement that involves extending relaxed hanging arms while twisting towards the thumb.

Pulling arm cycles. Arm cycles in which the elbows move backwards immediately after key depression.

Pulling arm legato. Use of pulling arm cycles (combined with either pronating or supinating circles) to play long, minimally separated tones.

Pulling finger. One of two basic finger strokes in which the fingertips, coming from an extended position, move under towards the palm to create backward friction with the keys.

Pulling midjoint touch. A seldom-used pulling touch in which the knuckle bone of the finger (first phalanx) retains a straight line with the hand while the midjoint alone flexes to activate a squeezing stroke; the nail joint, not flexing, bends backward.

Pushing arm cycles. Recurring arm cycles in which the elbows move forward immediately before and after key depression as the fingers slide forward on the keys.

Pushing finger. Identical to the unfolding finger coordination: fingertips extend away from the palms, propelled only by the small muscles in the hand.

Rebounds. Controlled after-tremors of a forearm gravity drop produced with the entire forearm. Hand rebounds are also possible.

Released to the outside. An important idea affecting the shoulders which, in good posture, are relaxed outward (and downward); this helps to stabilize the torso-neck-head unit and to free upper-arm movement in the shoulders.

Resting position. A comfortable, balanced position of the hand and arm (wrists are high) in which 1s and 5s play in palm position with middle fingers tucked under.

Rotation. A primary movement coordination in which the arms twist back and forth. A single rotation is made up of a pronation followed by a returning supination; the opposite order is also possible.

Scoop chord. A prepared chord played with actively scooping hands backed by quickly pressing forearms.

Scoop pressure. A gentle and sustained graded pressure, generated by scooping hands and pulling arms, which is employed to back a pulling finger legato.

Shoulder girdle. A yokelike structure, made up of collarbones and shoulder blades, representing the first link in the piano-playing chain.

Sidesaddle position. A position of the body turned half right or half left of center that allows the hand near the keyboard to play sideways with its knuckles perpendicular to the fallboard.

Sidesaddle two-finger walking. An exercise in sidesaddle posture calling for two fingers to alternate as they play a legato scale up and down the keyboard.

Signpost notes. Ds and G♯s: these notes are coincident when playing a contrary chromatic scale beginning on middle D; they are named for their distance from middle D.

Small finger muscles. The finger muscles located in the hand controlling the first phalanx of the finger. These muscles, working alone, generate the unfolding finger coordination, during which wrists are loose and generally high.

Sostenuto pedal. The middle pedal, capable of automatically sustaining predetermined tones.

Squeezing finger. A pulling coordination of the finger in which a prepared extended finger is pulled under purely by the action of the small finger muscles working on the first phalanx; the other joints, not flexing at all, bend backwards.

Substitution practice. A legato exercise for finger nimbleness in which the same finger is able to play each new scale note because its neighbor has substituted for it to facilitate a legato connection.

Supinated stretches. A less strenuous way for fingers to stretch lateral distance on the keyboard. A supinated position of the hand and arm allows flexing movements of the fingers to cover lateral keyboard distance; useful in spread chords and spread legato passages.

Supinating circles (cycles). Recurring arm cycles in which the elbows go inward immediately after key depression.

Supination. Twisting the arm outwards in the direction of the fifth finger.

Three-octave D. The Ds three octaves on either side of middle D.

Thumb midjoint. The joint connecting the mid- or second phalanx of the thumb to its palm bone. In claw position it is out and back.

Topography. Term used to denote the irregular shape of the keyboard.

Torso-neck-head alignment. A structural entity of the body which remains intact when posture is correct, and which forms the basis for healthy, efficient movement.

Trajectory. A given path of movement.

Trombone-slide diagonal. A straight-line diagonal approach to the keyboard usually resulting from a forearm push stroke; upper arms move forward to support the stroke.

Two and a half-octave G♯. The G♯s two and a half octaves on either side of middle D.

Two octave D. The Ds two octaves on either side of middle D.

Two-tier system. The keyboard is arranged in two tiers: the higher, black-key level and the lower, white-key level.

Ulna knob. The bony protuberance on the outside of the forearm near the wrist.

Una corda **pedal.** The left or soft pedal.

Unfolding finger. One of two basic finger coordinations in which the fingertips move (unfold) outward, away from the palms of the hands.

Upper-arm gravity drop. A coordination in which the upper arms, falling in the shoulders, propel the fingers into the keys. There are two forms of this coordination: high wrist and low wrist. Both forms create backward friction with the keys.

Vibrato pedal. Fast, tiny movements of the pedal at the engagement point, producing a continuously pedaled sonority with relative clarity.

Washboard motion. A small vertical back-and-forth movement of the hands and extended arms along the trombone-slide diagonal.

White area. The near third of the keyboard covering the wide part of the white keys.

Suggestions for Further Reading

Many of the following works are totally devoted to the subject of piano technique and its pedagogy. In others, technical matters come up as part of a larger orientation, such as piano study, piano playing, or psychology and the like, but they also contain excellent technical insights and suggestions. I recommend this list of interesting and worthwhile books to those who wish to pursue further study.

Bacon, Ernst. 1963. *Notes on the Piano.* Syracuse, NY: Syracuse University Press.

Bardas, Willy. 1982. *On the Psychology of Piano Technique.* Trans. Robert Lilienfeld. Brooklyn, NY: Beechwood Press.

Bernstein, Seymour. 1981. *With Your Own Two Hands.* New York: Schirmer Books.

Bonpensiere, Luigi. 1952. *New Pathways to Piano Technique.* New York: Philosophical Library.

Caplan, Deborah. 1987. *Back Trouble.* Gainesville, FL: Triad Publishing.

Chase, Mildred Portney. 1985. *Just Being at the Piano.* Berkeley: Creative Arts Books.

Ching, James. 1946. *Piano Playing.* (25 lectures). London: Bosworth.

———. 1962. *On Teaching Piano Technique to Children.* London: Keith Prowse.

Curcio, Louise. 1975. *Space Playing.* Newark, NJ: Modern Pianistics.

Deutsch, Leonhard. 1959. *Guided Sight-Reading: A New Approach to Piano Study.* Chicago: Nelson-Hall.

Everhart, Powell. 1958. *The Pianists Art; A Comprehensive Manual on Piano-Playing for the Student and Teacher.* Atlanta, GA: Powell Everhart.

Fielden, Thomas. 1927. *The Science of Pianoforte Technique.* London: Macmillan.

Gat, Jozsef. 1965. *The Techniques of Piano Playing.* Trans. Istvan Kleszky. 4th ed. London: Collet's Holdings.

Gerig, Reginald R. 1974. *Famous Pianists and Their Technique.* Washington: Robert B. Luce.

Gieseking, Walter, and Karl Leimer. 1972. *Piano Technique.* New York: Dover.

Green, Barry, with Timothy Galway. 1986. *The Inner Game of Music.* New York: Anchor Press.

Herrigel, Eugen. 1953. *Zen in the Art of Archery.* New York: Pantheon Books.

Huntley, Noel. 1982. *The Hidden Variables of Piano Technique and the Fundamentals of Skill.* Los Angeles, CA: Prescience Publications.

Kentner, Louis. 1976. *The Piano.* New York: Schirmer Books.

Kochevitsky, George. 1967. *The Art of Piano Playing: A Scientific Approach.* Evanston, IL: Summy-Birchard.

Matthay, Tobias A. 1932. *The Visible and Invisible in Piano Technique.* New York: Oxford University Press.

Neuhaus, Heinrich. 1973. *The Art of Piano Playing.* Trans. K. A. Leibovitch. New York: Praeger.

Noyle, Linda J., ed. 1987. *Pianists on Playing: Interviews With Twelve Concert Pianists.* Metuchen, NJ: Scarecrow Press.

Ortmann, Otto. 1962. *The Physiological Mechanics of Piano Technique.* 2nd ed., paperback reprint. New York: E. P. Dutton.

Pichier, Paul, and Walter Krause. 1972. *The Pianist's Touch.* Trans. Martha Ideler. Marshall, CA: Perelen Publishing.

Further Reading

Ristad, Eloise. 1982. *A Soprano on Her Head.* Utah: Real People Press.

Sandor, Gyorgy. 1981. *On Piano Playing: Motion, Sound and Expression.* New York: Schirmer Books.

Schultz, Arnold. 1936. *The Riddle of the Pianist's Finger.* Boston: Carl Fischer.

Taylor, Kendall. 1981. *Principles of Piano Technique and Interpretation.* Borough Green, Kent: Novello.

Taylor, Harold. 1979. *The Pianist's Talent.* London: Kahn and Averill.

Whiteside, Abbey. 1955. *Indispensables of Piano Playing.* New York: Scribner.

Wilson, Frank R. 1987. *Tone Deaf and All Thumbs.* New York: Vintage Books.

Yates, Peter. 1964. *An Amateur at the Keyboard.* New York: Random House.

Index

Arch (knuckle level) 42, 44, 49, 78, 83, 110, 116, 123-124, 129-130, 132

Arm (*See also* Forearm, Upper arm) 22, 24-35, 45-52, 56, 76-95

    cycling 28, 29-30, 50-52, 78-81, 107, 127-128, 132, 134, 156-158, 168-170

    extension 24, 25-26, 31-32

    flexion 33, 46-47

    gesturing 152-155

    joggle movement 142-147

    lateral movement 19, 33-35, 56, 62, 101, 116-117, 160-162, 163-164

    multi-note patterns 90, 111, 132-133, 144, 148-151, 152-155

    parallel motion 165-167

    pronation 24-25, 29-32, 46-47, 78-79, 152

    pulling 27, 42, 43, 50, 76, 78-81, 86, 87-89, 142

    pushing 24, 25, 31-32, 44, 45, 52, 60, 76, 83-84, 143

    rotation 18, 24-25, 48-49

    supination 29, 80-81, 90-92, 93-95, 124-125

    weight transfer 90-91, 111, 130, 152-158, 168-170

Arpeggios 13, 35, 115, 130, 160, 168-170

Aural image (inner hearing) 11, 12, 13, 14, 69, 131

Balance and equilibrium 13, 24, 33-35, 55-58, 59, 92, 101, 160-162, 165, 168

Balistic impulse 26, 35, 87-88, 98-100, 101, 102-103, 106-107 163-165, 168-170, 172

Bilateral symmetry (even-sided development) 13, 20, 22-23, 31, 39, 58, 98, 101, 107, 165

Black keys 20, 57-59, 60, 61, 62-63, 101, 119, 159

Central position and orientation 53, 58, 59, 66, 101

Chords 41, 45, 83-86, 87-88, 110-111, 146-147, 157, 159, 162

Choreography (dancer-athlete) 11, 14-15, 23, 34, 59-60, 66, 90-93, 152-158, 168-170, 177

Chromatic scale 58

Chromatic transposition 59-60, 65

Claw position 37, 44, 48, 110, 114, 116, 129, 143, 146, 174-175

Continuity (physical and musical) 50, 55, 76, 78, 90-95, 111, 117, 126-128, 152, 168

Contrary (mirrored) motion 13, 22-23, 57, 58-59, 62, 66, 75, 111, 113, 165

Correspondence (alignment) 96-99, 118, 126

Creativity in performance (expression) 11, 13-15, 23, 46, 50, 52, 60, 66, 69, 117, 127, 131, 141, 143, 176-177

Cyclical movements 29-31, 49, 52, 78-81, 90, 107, 116-117, 129, 152-154, 156-157, 160-161, 168-170

Damper pedal 66-68

Efficiency of movement 23, 34, 50, 54-56, 71, 74, 85, 91, 94, 96

Elbows 32, 33, 49, 78, 80, 96, 117, 152-153

Extended position 36, 42, 58, 76, 80, 119, 130, 159

Fatigue 40, 42, 108, 152, 163-164, 166, 174

Fifth finger 49, 80-81, 98, 123-125, 132-134, 135, 158

Figure-eight adjustments 34, 100, 107, 117, 126-127

Finger-interval bonding (hand vocabulary) 58, 59-60, 64-66, 110, 168-169

Fingering procedures 57, 58-60, 66, 135, 148, 154, 168-169

Fingers 13, 16, 36-45, 118-135

    height adjustments 63, 148, 159

    independence 39, 42, 45, 118, 159, 173

    length adaptations 158-160

    looseness 58, 61, 142, 146-147

    position 36-38, 48-49, 60-61, 64, 96-98, 132, 148, 158

    preset 40, 78, 80, 83, 96, 102-103, 106-107, 110, 130, 148-149, 163, 171

    pulling 38-39, 41, 42-43, 111, 118-122, 159

    finger snap stroke 113, 120, 148-149, 168, 171-173

        midjoint stroke 159

        scratching stroke 121

        squeezing stroke 119

        unprepared stroke 122

    release 113, 131, 173-175

    stretching 93-94

    timing 102, 113

    unfolding 38-39, 44-45, 129, 132, 172

        finger spring stroke 45, 131

Flexibility 12, 13, 14, 34, 48-50, 55-57, 66, 75, 80, 90-95, 116-117, 152-154, 156-157, 160-161

Forearm 31-35, 96-105, 148-151

    bounce stroke 96-99

    flexion 31-33, 39, 46-47, 96, 148

    gravity drops 102, 148, 163

    push stroke 31-32, 83, 96, 143, 146-147

    pronation 25, 29-30, 34, 48-49, 93

    rebounds 102-103, 163-165

Index

supination 25, 29-30, 34, 48-49, 91-92, 123
Forearm-finger grouping 148-152
   forenotes 151

Gesturing (arm) 152-158
Grasping stroke 113

Habit formation 14, 23-24, 30, 39, 45, 54, 59,
   96-98, 114, 132
Hand 36-38, 106-109
   bounce stroke 106-108, 163-165
   calisthenics 39, 50
   flexion 40-41, 106
   lateral movement 19, 34, 78, 80, 90-94, 97,
      100, 101, 127, 152
   positions 36-37, 39, 48, 60, 100, 110, 132
   rebounds 107, 163-165
   release 171
   scoop stroke 40-41, 152
Hand-finger staccato 171-173
Hand scoop pressure 43, 111, 152
Hand vocabulary 58, 59-60, 64-66, 110,
   168-169

Individual differences 75
Integrative movements 24, 46-52, 54-56,
   90-94, 116-117, 131, 142-146, 148, 171,
   176
Isometrics 40-41, 42-44, 50

Joggle movement 142-147

Karate position 80, 123
Key
   backward friction 40, 42, 43, 50, 78, 79, 106
   forward friction 32, 44, 52, 83, 102, 129
   weight 45, 58, 61, 129, 132, 173
Keybedding 86, 102, 122, 142-43
Keyboard 20, 57-66
   address and position 46, 53-57
   anomalies 57-58, 59
   depth-zone areas 20, 57, 62
   middle D 58
   strategy 56, 58-60, 61
   two-tiered system 57, 63, 66
   typography (shape) 46, 48-49, 50, 57, 62-63,
      66
Kinesthetic signals 13, 14, 41, 46, 47, 49, 56,
   61, 85, 107
Knuckle joint (See also Arch) 34, 42, 49, 98,
   100, 123-124, 143, 159

Lateral motion 33-35, 55, 56, 57, 101, 116-117,
   132, 160-162, 163-165, 168-170
Learning 14-15, 22, 23, 30, 39, 48, 53, 58, 140,
   177

Left foot 55, 56
Legato 41, 43, 45, 67, 78, 111, 126, 146
   fake 168-170
   joggle 142-146
   overlapping 126, 148
Legato pedal (syncopated) 67
Listening 68, 69
Looseness 24, 30-31, 49, 78, 80, 87-88,
   107-112, 142, 145-146, 163

Mental interference 14, 22, 23, 30, 39, 48, 145,
   146
Middle D 20, 53, 58,
Musical continuity and line 11, 52, 55, 61,
   77-78, 80, 90-94, 116-117, 126-127, 145,
   152, 160, 168-170

Neck 24, 54

Octaves 166-167

Palm position 37, 88, 96-97, 106, 113, 116,
   121, 123, 131, 148, 163
Parallel movement 59, 165-167
Pedals 54, 66-70
Pendulum swing 27
Playing apparatus 13, 22, 45-46, 50, 57, 74-75,
   130-131, 176
Posture 13, 24, 27, 46, 48, 53-54, 71, 101, 132,
   165-166
Practice 13-14, 22-23, 26, 30, 39, 54, 68, 86,
   132, 161-162
Primary movements 13, 14, 22, 45
   arms 24-35
   fingers 36-45
   hands 36-41
Pronation (arm) 18, 24, 25, 34, 46, 98
Pulling finger stroke 42-43, 118-122
Pulling arm cycle (See also Arms) 50, 78-81,
   87, 152
Pull/push cycles 90, 107, 171
Pulsation 50, 76, 78, 80, 90-94, 164-165, 176
Pushing arm cycle (See also Arms) 52, 83,
   90-94, 152

Rebounds 102-103, 163-165
Resonance 66, 67, 69
Resting position 100, 102, 163-164, 171
Right foot 54, 66
Rotation 24, 28, 29-31, 48, 152
Rounded palm position of fingers 37, 42, 44, 98

Scale playing 13, 35, 58, 59, 115, 148, 153,
   172, 174
Scoop chords 40, 110
Scoop pressure 41, 111, 142, 152

"Seeing" with relaxed fingers 61, 64
Shoulders
    blades 26
    elliptical circles 55
    released to the outside 24, 27, 55
Shoulder girdle 13, 17, 27, 46-47
    cycles 34, 50-52, 76, 78-82, 83-86, 90-94, 117,
        142, 152
    lateral movement 33, 62, 117, 160
Sidesaddle practice 132-134
Small finger muscles 38, 45, 106, 119, 129, 132
Sostenuto pedal 70
Speed (velocity) 23, 30, 50-51, 91, 101, 103,
        107, 142, 148, 152, 163, 171
Staccato 83, 96, 106, 120, 121, 163, 171
Straight-line motion 31-32, 34, 96, 101, 148,
        163
Strength (power) 25, 45, 78, 80, 83, 87, 96,
        102, 110, 142, 143, 163, 171
Substitution practice 135
Supination (arm) 18, 24, 29, 34, 49, 80, 91, 94,
        117

Tension (See also Fatigue) 41, 42, 58, 86, 88,
        102, 163-166, 171, 174
Thumbs 17, 42, 48, 78, 98-99, 112-117, 126
    grasping stroke 113
    lateral movement 114, 115, 116-117
    palm-bone retraction 37, 39, 114
    palm position 98-99, 106
    in scale and arpeggio playing 115
    vertical movement 112-113
Tone quality 66-67, 69-70, 76, 126, 142, 168,
        171-172, 173-175
Topography of the keyboard 57-66
Torso-neck-head alignment 24, 54, 55
Transposition 58-59, 64-65
Tremolo 31
Trombone-slide motion 31, 96, 102, 129, 148,
        163, 171

Una corda pedal 69-70
Underlying rhythm (See Pulsation)
Unfolding finger stoke 44-45, 129, 132, 168,
        173
Upper arms (See also Arms) 24-33, 45-52,
        76-95
    gesturing 152-156
    individual key depressions 76-77, 78-89,
        142-144
    lateral motion 19, 34, 117, 101, 160-162
    as prime mover 26, 45, 50, 136
    pulling gravity cycles 76-80
    pushing cycles 76, 83-85

Velocity (See Speed)

Warm-up 15, 45
Washboard motion 32, 60-61, 96, 148, 163
Weight transfer 90-91, 111, 117, 126-128, 131,
        132-134, 153, 168-170
White keys 20, 57, 63, 132, 158
Wrist
    in figure-eight (lateral) movement 34, 78-81,
        90-94, 98, 119-122, 126-128, 160, 163,
        168
    in high position 96, 100, 102, 129, 143, 163
    as pneumatic gear 85, 87, 88, 110, 142, 152,
        171
    in pulling legato 41-42, 110, 152
    in vertical hand movement 40, 106, 143, 152,
        164